YOUR A–Z GUIDE TO THE STOCK MARKET

AND ALL YOU NEED TO KNOW ABOUT CAPITAL TERMS

Rajen Devadason

TIMES BOOKS INTERNATIONAL
Singapore • Kuala Lumpur

© 1997 Rajen Devadason

Published by Times Books International
an imprint of Times Editions Pte Ltd
Times Centre
1 New Industrial Road
Singapore 536196
Fax: (65) 2854871 Tel: (65) 2848844
e-mail: te@corp.tpl.com.sg

Times Subang
Lot 46, Subang Hi-Tech Industrial Park
Batu Tiga
40000 Shah Alam
Selangor Darul Ehsan
Malaysia
Fax & Tel: (603) 7363517

All rights reserved. No part of this publication may be reproduced, stored in a retrieval system or transmitted, in any form or by any means, electronic, mechanical, phocopying, recording or otherwise, without the prior permission of the copyright owner.

Printed in Singapore

ISBN 981 204 744 1

This book is dedicated to my mother, Mrs Janaki Devadason, who believes in me intensely and prays so earnestly that there may be hope yet for me, and to my father, Mr Daniel Devadason, who urged me to write books.

ACKNOWLEDGEMENTS

My deepest thanks to my sister, Viji, for allowing her freeloading brother to set up office in her house; P. Gunasegaram, Head of Research at Leong and Co., who first taught me how to work out a **PE** ratio and has been educating me ever since; Tan Teng Boo, managing director of Capital Dynamics, who introduced me to the concepts of prudent investing and to the name 'Warren **Buffett**'; S. Jayasankaran of the **Far Eastern Economic Review** for guiding me through the maze that is corporate Malaysia and making me realise how much fun could be had doing so; Ahmad Kushairi Mohd Lotfi of Nava SC Securities Research (Malaysia) who supplied me with several pages of conventional **investment** terms and definitions; Edwin Chong, a top-notch, honest **remisier** with OSK Securities, who did the same for highly unconventional terms; Michael Greenall, research director of Caspian Securities in Malaysia, for help on an earlier list of the Dow stocks and for always going out of his way to be a friend; Dave Tan who told me about **Reminiscences of a Stock Operator** and whose razor-sharp logic has constantly kept me on my toes; K. Sree Kumar, executive director of Kaf-Refco Futures Sdn Bhd, for explaining the arcane world of financial **futures** to me; Tong Kooi Ong and Rudy Koh of Phileo Allied Bank who were friends and teachers long before they became bank-owning tycoons; John Duggan, chief operating officer of **KLOFFE**, who was patient enough to repeatedly explain things that were crystal clear to him but opaque to me until even I understood the issues involved; Fred Tam who provided me an education by just watching him bounce

Acknowledgements

back with a vengeance from setbacks that would have floored lesser men; Susan Chan of **Malaysian Business** magazine for introducing me to Christine Chong of Times Editions; Christine Chong for commissioning this book, thank you for making a dream come true.

Also, Christine Chua, senior editor at Times Editions, for bearing with my many delays, excuses of tardiness and computer malfunctions; if you aren't too fed up, perhaps we can do this again sometime? Special thanks to Lim Kwee Lan and Shova Loh of Times Editions for caring enough to go the second mile.

My bosses and colleagues, past and present, at my biggest client *Smart Investor* magazine for allowing me time off for this project – Jason Hoong, Ricky Ang, Chong Huai Seng, Agatha Koh, A.J. Leow, Carol Lo, Daniel Goh and Peter Loh.

On a more personal note, Rachel Tan, Steven Poh and Ahmad Rejal Arbee for invaluable support, friendship and understanding, and especially Benjamin Yeoh and Pang Chok Hin who helped make this book a reality through ways tangible and otherwise.

To all of these and the many I've inadvertently left out (and who will hound me because of that), thank you.

PREFACE

If you dread the idea of heading off to your next class reunion because of all the insufferable oafs from school who will make chauffeured entrances in mountain-sized Mercs or, worse yet, drive themselves in flashy Ferraris, take heart. This book is for you.

Nothing in here will, in the short-term at least, facilitate any massive auto upgrade. However, when the general conversation at your reunion turns to high finance and **investment**s you will more than just hold your own. Just make sure a copy of this book is tucked somewhere discreetly on your person. First, this is what you need to do. Buy this book. Or if you're already a follower of **Arkad's Cure 2 for a Lean Purse** (see entry) then better still, borrow a copy of *Your A–Z Guide to the Stock Market* from a friend.

This book has been designed as a self-referential primer of words, phrases and even names related to the stock markets and economies of the world, in general, and Southeast Asia, in particular. It also delves unashamedly into principles and philosophies of saving and investing. The self-referential bit means that you can look up terms highlighted in bold elsewhere in the book for a clearer view of the big picture.

It deals with concepts like **depreciation** and **passive investment strategies** while giving you formulae for complex things like **future value** and **CAGR**. On top of all that, it will finally explain to you the difference between a **bond**, a **share**, an **option** and a **T-bill**, or a company's **EPS**, **PE** and **NAV**. Truly important stuff that you have undoubtedly been losing sleep over.

But *Your A–Z Guide to the Stock Market*'s greatest help may well materialise when the conversation near you takes a nosedive and you need a quick joke or unheard of word to astound and entertain those around you. Should that happen, run into the restroom, retrieve your copy of this book from wherever you deposited it on your anatomy, and look up the references for **Noah** and **chrometophobia**. Just be careful someone else in the gathering hasn't beaten you to it. This book will also help you decipher what that desperate chap with the lean, haunted look in the corner really means when he asks you, "**What's the news?**" Even if you haven't heard any (rumours, that is) you can regale him with your lucid definitions of a **quant, chartist** and **dog**. Or you could astound him with your sophisticated monologue on the dangers of **window dressing** and then snicker at him with a superior air as he begins to look in puzzlement at the curtains.

In whatever way you utilise this book, I hope you find *Your A–Z Guide to the Stock Market* entertaining and profitable. If it is the latter, do drop me a line c/o Times Editions, the address is at the beginning of the book. I'd love a ride in your new Ferrari.

Rajen Devadason
May, 1997

A

A
The single letter code for Attwoods, a company listed on the **NYSE**. (See **stock symbol**.)

abnormal rate of return
A common perception of the **risk-return** relationship is that if more risk is taken, greater **return**s must ensue. An abnormal rate of return is that happy exception where returns are above what can normally be expected for a specified amount of **risk**.

absorption
A **takeover** of the most overwhelming sort. The absorbed company is gobbled up by the absorbing one, which takes over all its **asset**s. In digesting its prey, the marauder liquidates the legal entity that was once a **company** in its own right.

accelerated earnings
The case of a company's earnings, not merely increasing, but seeing its rate of increase rise with time. For instance, Company A with **EPS** figures of 20 cents, 24 cents and 28 cents, over a three-year period can boast of rising earnings but certainly not accelerated

earnings, since EPS growth between Year 1 and Year 2 is 20%, slowing down to 17% between Year 2 and Year 3.

In contrast, Company B with EPS figures of 20 cents, 22 cents and 26 cents, most certainly has both rising earnings and accelerated earnings, 10% followed by 18% in terms of EPS growth. As a rule, a company with accelerated earnings deserves a premium **P/E** rating. (See **Lynch's Rule**.)

account

Most generally, a record of financial dealings within a set period. Therefore both a **P&L** and a **balance sheet** would be examples of an account. (See also **financial statements**.)

The term is also used to describe a contractual relationship between a **dealer** or **remisier** and a client which allows for buy and sell transactions with delayed settlement.

accumulated tax credits

The sum of unused **tax credits** a **company** currently possesses. (See **accumulated tax losses**.)

accumulated tax losses

Although no company enjoys being in a loss-making situation, one advantage of having a bad spell with **red ink** flowing over several years is the corresponding accumulation of those losses which can be used to reduce the tax charge in the first few years a profit is chalked up.

For instance, let's look at company Slow Start, that we assume operates in a country where the corporate tax rate is 30%. Slow Start loses $30m in its first year of operations and $5m in its second. In its third year it makes $10m and in its fourth $200m. The bad years add up to accumulated losses of $35m. These losses are looked upon by the pleasant gentlemen in that country's inland revenue department as **accumulated tax credits**. These credits fully offset the profit of the third year so no tax is payable. $10m worth of credits is exhausted in offsetting the profit of Year 3, leaving $25m in unutilised accumulated tax losses. In the fourth, bonanza, year when Slow Start makes a pre-tax profit of $200m, the tax department will offset that by the remaining tax credits, leaving $175m to be hit by the 30% tax charge. For that year the company's taxes come to $52.5m (30% of $175m, not 30% of $200m).

Note that because of the gradual utilisation of the accumulated tax credits, the **effective tax rate** of Slow Start in Year 3 is 0%, and in Year 4 it is 26.25% (that is, 100% **x** 52.5m/200m). When analysing companies for potential **investment** worthiness it is important to look out for peculiarly low effective tax rates and to determine if and when accumulated tax losses run out. Usually when they are fully exhausted, a company's **EPS** will take a battering. (See **taxation**.)

acid-test ratio

A relatively quick way to ascertain the sufficiency of **liquid assets** of a business. It is calculated by dividing the total cash, short-term **securities**, and accounts receivable or short-term debtors by **current liabilities** (those due within a year).

This essentially collapses into the following formula:

$$\text{acid-test ratio} = \frac{\{\text{current assets} - (\text{inventory and work-in-progress})\}}{\text{current liabilities}}$$

The larger the ratio the better shape the business is in to meet its immediate obligations. Ideally, a company should boast an acid-test ratio of more than 1 to appear attractive by this yardstick.

active investment strategy

An extremely hands-on investment strategy where the owner or manager of a **portfolio** constantly looks at price movements and unceasingly adjusts the proportions of the constituent assets in it.

The danger with having too active an investment strategy is that commission charges build up, undoing much of the benefits of **compounding**, while the possibility of making wrong moves through excessive trading rises. The advantage though is that there should be sufficient **diversification** of **asset**s arising from this strategy to minimise the overall portfolio loss from a drop in the prices of one asset class.

ADRs
American depository receipts.

advance-decline line
A line graph showing the number of stocks that rose against the number that fell in a particular period.

aggressive stock
A stock with a **beta** greater than 1.0. (See **defensive stock**.)

AGM
Annual General Meeting.

All Mining
A secondary index of the Australian Stock Exchange. (See also **All Ordinaries**.)

All Ordinaries
The Australian Stock Exchange's **benchmark index**. (See also **All Mining**.)

All Ordinaries
A secondary index of the **Hong Kong Stock Exchange**. (See also **Hang Seng Index** and **Dow Jones (HK) Small Cap**.)

all or none
Specific instructions to a **dealer** from a client to either buy all of a specified order, say 100 **lot**s of ABC Ltd, or none at all. If the dealer only manages to locate the sellers of 97 lots, the client does not want them.

allotment
The allocation of new securities to a subscriber. As is commonly the case, when the issue is oversubscribed allotment is done through balloting.

All Shares Price Index
The Colombo Stock Exchange's **benchmark index**. (See also **Sensitive Price Index**.)

alpha
When utilising the capital asset pricing model (**CAPM**), it is possible to deduce a linear relationship between the expected **return** on an **investment** and its **risk**. The risk portion of this equation is called the **beta**. Because the CAPM is an equilibrium model, any investor is free to forecast a rate of return on an **asset** in excess of that predicted by the CAPM. This excess is called the alpha. Over a long period it is possible to empirically determine the actual historical alpha of a stock. If this value is positive, the stock is a good investment with returns exceeding what can generally be expected from an investment with the same risk profile.

Amanah Saham Bumiputera
A Malaysian unit trust reserved for **bumiputras**, run by **PNB**, launched in April 1981.

Amanah Saham Nasional
Another Malaysian unit trust reserved for **bumiputras**, run by **PNB**, launched in January 1990 as an extension to **ASB**.

Amanah Saham Wawasan 2020
A Malaysian unit trust that is 51% reserved for **bumiputras** and 49% for other Malaysians, run by **PNB**. It is a **closed-end** fund that targets young Malaysians. It was open to all those who were between 12 and 29 years old during the one-month application window in late 1996.

American depository receipts
ADRs. Receipts for chunks of foreign shares held in a US-based bank. These aggregated receipts can be bought and sold by US investors wanting ready, uncomplicated exposure to foreign equities.

American Stock Exchange Composite Index
Benchmark index for **AMEX**.

AMEX
American Stock Exchange, a smaller, less demanding cousin of the **NYSE**. It contains smaller and, many would say, more speculative stocks than the NYSE. It has five supporting member exchanges, namely the Boston, Chicago, Cincinnati, Pacific and Philadelphia exchanges.

analyst
A born ferret who lives to discover hidden value in companies or to unearth a profound reason to dump them. This is done through an often imprecise combination of primary research and intricate spreadsheet building, secondary discussion and tertiary gut feel. Analysts are widely thought to be overpaid, particularly when the general remuneration packages of relatively young analysts are compared to the money made by even much older general managers of large companies.

This however is merely another example of **demand and supply** rearing its head. The bottom line is that pay scales and contribution to society seldom go hand in hand. Consider the pittance made by nurses or teachers against the inflation-inducing pay cheques of analysts and dealers. Having said that, it is nonetheless arguable that analysts more than earn their keep by judiciously providing constipated dealers a chance to vent the venom built up from having to be suck up to potential clients, particularly **institutional investors**.

Annualised Percentage Rate

APR. The real interest on a loan expressed as a simple annual percentage. The APR allows varying loan packages to be compared on an equal footing to help those hunting around for the cheapest loan to make sound decisions.

annual report and accounts

Masterpieces of presentation that allow a **savvy investor** a chance to determine if a **company** is worth the paper its story is printed on. The presence of an auditor's stamp of approval gives slightly more credence to these than the material being spewed out by the company's public relations department.

annual total return

The total gain from an **investment** including **capital gain** and **dividend** income for the period. (See **paper profit**.)

annuity

A periodic, regular income derived from a contract sold by an insurance company to provide security for life. In a broader, much looser sense, blue chip stocks that pay regular dividends can be looked upon as annuity instruments too.

APB

Asia Pacific Fund.

appreciation

Just as every person seeks this in interpersonal relationships, every **investor** looks for this in his **portfolio**, to keep it ballooning. More specifically, it is the increase in an asset's current price over the original purchase price.

APR

Annualised Percentage Rate. (See also **usury**.)

arbitrage

The simultaneous purchase and sale of an **investment** instrument in two distinct exchanges where a price differential exists due to an inefficient flow of information. For instance, if gold is selling for US$350 an ounce in New York and the equivalent of US$348 in Manila, a simultaneous purchase of a pound of it in the Philippines and a sale of a pound in the US would yield a gross arbitrage profit of US$32.

arbitrageur

A person who engages in **arbitrage**. He serves the common good since his very actions eliminate the inefficiency that caused the differential in the first place, and quite rightly makes money out of his service. Taking the example above, if an arbitrageur in Jakarta decides to buy enough gold over the phone in Manila, his activity will raise the price of gold a little – US$1, for instance. His simultaneous selling activity in the US might then depress the price of gold there by US$1, bringing equilibrium to the gold price.

Arkad

The Richest Man in Babylon, the title character of George Samuel **Clason**'s book on financial health that outlines sound money-linked principles such as **Seven Cures for a Lean Purse** and **Five Laws of Gold.** (Also see below for **Arkad's Cure 1** to **7 for a Lean Purse.**)

Arkad's Cure 1 for a Lean Purse

Start thy purse to fattening. (See **Clason, George Samuel.**)

Arkad's Cure 2 for a Lean Purse

Control thy expenditures. (See **Clason, George Samuel.**)

Arkad's Cure 3 for a Lean Purse

Make thy gold multiply. (See **Clason, George Samuel.**)

Arkad's Cure 4 for a Lean Purse
Guard thy treasures from loss. (See **Clason, George Samuel**.)

Arkad's Cure 5 for a Lean Purse
Make of thy dwelling a profitable investment. (See **Clason, George Samuel**.)

Arkad's Cure 6 for a Lean Purse
Ensure a future income. (See **Clason, George Samuel**.)

Arkad's Cure 7 for a Lean Purse
Increase thy ability to earn. (See **Clason, George Samuel**.)

articles of association
Because a **company** is a legal entity in its own right, these articles help stipulate the essential terms of agreement between **shareholders** and the company. They encompass virtually every aspect of incorporation including the management of the company, the issue of shares and the rights of shareholders. Every company has a set of articles of association as well as a **memorandum of association**. To be valid, both the articles and the memorandum must be in harmony with each other and also not be in conflict with any law of the land.

ASB
Amanah Saham Bumiputera.

ascending tops
Chartists use this term for a pattern, much like that of a rising mountain range, where the consecutive price peaks of a **stock**, say, describe a rising trend.

Asia Pacific Fund
Commonly denoted as **APB**. This **closed-end fund** is listed on the **NYSE** and was launched in April 1987 by Baring International. Its

stated investment objectives are to ride on the long-term capital growth of the entire Asia Pacific Rim. It tends to focus its investment activities in Hong Kong, Malaysia, the Philippines, Singapore, South Korea, Taiwan and Thailand. Price and **NAV** data on **APB** are readily found in the **AWSJ**. (See **mutual fund**.)

asked
Also called the **offer**. It is the lowest price a seller of an **asset** – be it a stock, car or state-owned bridge – is willing to take. This pairs off with a **bid** to give a single **quotation** and the corresponding **spread**.

ASN
Amanah Saham Nasional.

asset
Anything owned by you or owed to you that either has a monetary value today or will produce a flow of benefits tomorrow. It stands in diametric opposition to a **liability**. The crux of sound investing is to buy appreciating assets.

asset allocation
The 'wheels' on the 'cart' of **diversification**. It involves the splitting up of investment funds between different categories of assets. A simple form of asset allocation is to have 40% of your net wealth tied up in your home, 40% in the **stock market** and 20% in the bank.

asset play
A stock investment that appears attractive not primarily for its earnings potential but rather for its underlying asset base. Property counters are often prime cases of asset plays.

asset stripper
A person (usually male) who indulges in **asset stripping**. (See **White Knight**.)

asset stripping
The process of a corporate predator breaking up a company, group or **conglomerate** piecemeal in the hope of making a quick, hefty profit from the sale of its components.

associate
A company not more than half-owned (usually between 20% and 50% held) by a **parent company** above it in the group hierarchy. (See **subsidiary**.)

'a sure thing'
Ain't no such thing in this **investment** game. The best you can do is study the odds as rationally as you know how, then try and stack them in your favour.

ASW 2020
Amanah Saham Wawasan 2020.

asymmetric hedging strategy
A hedging strategy that puts a cap on the downside risk of loss of an **investment**. It is asymmetric however because it does not have a corresponding cap on the upside, therefore leaving the investor with the pleasant possibility of large, upside gains. (See **symmetric hedging strategy.**)

at discretion
Blanket permission given to a **dealer** or **remisier** by a client to put through a transaction at whatever price level and in whatever quantity the dealer deems fit. This sort of latitude should only be given to a dealer you trust implicitly but is useful in times of great volatility as it is the dealer who is in constant touch with the **market**.

at market
Executing a **market order**.

19

at the close
Specific instructions to a **dealer** from a client to complete a transaction just as a **market** closes.

at the market
See **at market**.

at-the-money option
This situation arises when the **exercise price** or **strike price** of the **option** is exactly equal to the current market price of the **underlying investment**. It is important to realise that this does not take into account the cost of the option itself. For instance, if an option is trading at $1.20 and its strike price is $3.80, it is considered an at the-money option when the underlying investment is trading at $3.80 (not $5.00).

at the opening
Specific instructions to a **dealer** from a client to complete a transaction just as a **market** opens.

Australian Dollar
The Australian currency. (See **currencies**.)

authorised capital
nominal value x number of **authorised shares**.

authorised shares
The number of shares a company is legally allowed to have at any one time. This always either equals or exceeds the paid up shares of the company.

average down
Buying shares that are falling so as to literally bring down the average cost of acquisition. For instance, if one **lot** of company ABC Ltd is

originally bought at $4 a share, and then the entire market takes a tumble, and ABC along with it, although the **fundamentals** of the company are unchanged, then it might be wise to average down. Consider **Gray's Deadly Sin 3**.

If so, then if two more lots are bought at $3 a share, and two more at $2 a share, the total price of acquisition (leaving aside commissions for the ease of calculation) is (assuming a **board lot** size of 1,000 shares) = 1000 x $(1 x 4 + 2 x 3 + 2 x 2) = $14,000. This amount has bought 5 lots which works out to an average cost of $2.80 a share. This means that when ABC's share price recovers and rises to perhaps $6, the average profit per share then rises, from the $2 it would have been without the averaging down exercise, to $3.20.

averaging

Taking the mean acquisition cost. (See **averaging down**.)

averaging down

If an **investment** you are confident about starts to head **south** for no valid reason, but appears to be doing so in tandem with a general feeling of despondency on the part of **Mr Market** then it would appear a good time to buy more of it. In doing so, your average cost of acquisition goes down, hence the term 'averaging down'. For a simple example, see **average down**.

When the price of your investment recovers, you will make more money per share (or **option** or **bond**) than if you had not taken advantage of the temporary price weakness. (See **Gray's Deadly Sin 3**.)

AWAS

The Malay word for 'caution' that serves as the acronym for the **KLSE**'s Advanced Warning and Surveillance Unit.

AWSJ

The **Asian Wall Street Journal**, the definitive business paper of the Asian region. A daughter publication of the **Wall Street Journal**.

In addition to providing excellent news coverage of the various business arenas around the continent, its 'Money & Investing Section' is widely regarded as the most comprehensive of the various regional publications.

Just one tiny segment like its Closed-End Funds table contains up-to-date price and **NAV** information on many US-listed funds, including those that focus on various parts of the world. (For background information on some of the Asian ones see **APB, FPF, IGF, IF, JGF, KF, MF, SAF, SGF, TWN, TEMF, TC** and **TTF**.)

B

B
The single letter code for Barnes Group, a company listed on the NYSE. (See **stock symbol**.)

BA
Banker's Acceptance.

back-door listing
A method of gaining a **stock exchange** listing by a **company** that ordinarily would not meet all of that exchange's listing requirements such as a high, sustained profit track record. Should an unlisted company take over a listed one, it can then inject its businesses into its acquisition and effectively list itself in the place of the target company. (See **reverse takeover**.)

bad debts
The killer of many struggling businesses. Generally the debtors' position in a company's **account**s is an **asset**, since it constitutes money owed to the business. But when some debtors either choose to or are unable to pay their debts, this affects the cash flow of the company owed money. When bad debts get out of control the company will suffer.

Baht
The Thai currency. (See **currencies**.)

balance sheet
One of the two most important financial statements of a company. The balance sheet 'freezes' all of a company's assets, liabilities and equity, on a set date (usually the last day of its financial year) and takes a snapshot of what the company is worth in those terms. (See **P&L**.)

Banker's Acceptance
A short-term investment security instrument used to facilitate both import and export trades. It works in a similar fashion to an individual writing a cheque. A **BA** is issued by a large corporation and drawn on a bank with which the company maintains an account. If PQR Ltd has to pay a supplier $1m in a hurry, it could issue that amount in BAs. The bank keeps the BA, and extends the loan to PQR who then uses it to pay its supplier. PQR's bank which underwrites this BA issue would take a marginal deposit from PQR and stump out the rest of the money for the supplier. PQR would then have between one month and one year, depending on the BA tenure, to repay the balance outstanding on that BA issue. BAs are traded openly as short-term securities by market players like a **discount house**.

Bank Negara Malaysia
Malaysia's **central bank**.

Bank of England
The United Kingdom's **central bank**.

Bank of Thailand
Thailand's **central bank**.

base lending rate
Commonly abbreviated to **BLR**. Loosely, it is another term for the **prime rate** of a bank.

basis point
One percent of one percent. So in banking circles a one basis point increase in interest rates would be a jump from 8.07% to 8.08%, for instance.

Basle Accord
An international banking agreement that requires all banks around the world to maintain a capital adequacy ratio (**CAR**) of at least 8% of their risk-weighted assets. It derives its name from Basle, Switzerland, where the accord was hammered out.

BCR
benefit cost ratio.

bear
An investor who thinks the **stock market** will head **south**.

bear market
A falling **stock market**, usually over a protracted period stretching many months or years.

bear trap
A short-lived *bullish* turn of the market that quickly dies with the market heading south again. This will leave **investor**s and **speculator**s who bought in during the short-lived upturn, or bear trap, stuck. Many of these will be unwilling to liquidate being loath to transform their **paper loss**es into actual ones. (Note that an inversion of the situation could be called a 'bull trap', where a brief bearish turn of the market evaporates and traps **short seller**s when the **market** turns bullish again!) See graph on page 26.

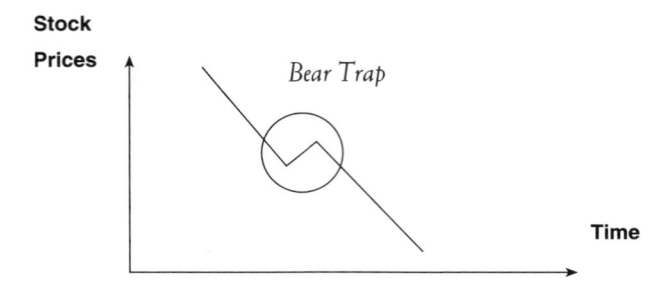

[Figure: Stock Prices vs Time, showing a declining line with a "Bear Trap" marked by a circled zigzag]

bell curve
Normal distribution curve or Gaussian distribution. (See standard deviation.)

benchmark index
The index most widely followed on a particular bourse and that is used by most investors as the primary barometer of activity on it. It is also the index against which fund managers measure their specific performances.

For example, in the US it would be the **DJIA** or **S&P 500**, in Singapore the **STII** and in Malaysia the **KLSE CI**. It is worth noting that in the US, the DJIA is the most closely followed index by the man on the street, but the more broadly representative S&P 500 is the benchmark that US fund managers tend to gauge their performance against.

benefit cost ratio
A single digit derived by summing all the cash inflows or benefits from a project of known duration; the same is done for all the costs over that same duration; then the **BCR** = total benefits/total costs. If the BCR is greater than 1.0 this generally means a project is deemed viable.

Berkshire Hathaway
Warren **Buffett**'s listed vehicle.

Bernama
Malaysia's national news agency.

beta
The systematic risk of a stock relative to the appropriate index. In Malaysia this would usually mean the KLSE CI, in Singapore, the Straits Times Industrial Index, and in Hong Kong the **Hang Seng Index**.

A beta value of 1.0 indicates that the stock moves in line with the index. Investors would buy beta =1 stocks if they wanted performance in line with the index.

A beta of more than one indicates greater volatility. Thus such a stock would shoot through the roof in a rising market, far faster than the overall market, and crash through the floor when the market starts to go down.

A beta of less than one indicates less volatility than the overall market. For instance, if the market falls or rises by 10%, the stock may only budge 5% in the same direction.

A negative beta value suggests negative correlation with the index. An investor's dream come true would be to be fully invested in negative beta stocks when the overall market, and thus the index, is plummeting. (See **risk-reward ratio** and **SML**.)

bid
The highest price a buyer of an **asset** – be it a commodity, truck or private yacht – is willing to pay. This pairs off with an **offer** or **asked** price to give a single **quotation** and the corresponding **spread**.

Big Bang
To astronomers this refers to the cataclysmic event that birthed the expanding universe. The term was borrowed by the British for an

27

explosive event on October 27, 1986, during Margaret Thatcher's watch as Prime Minister, when banks were allowed, for the first time in the UK, to participate in stockbroking activities. This was part of the British government's move toward greater deregulation and increased competitiveness.

big bath
When a company's **board** decides to take on extremely painful write downs in that year's **P&L** in a bid to clean things up for greater recovery in the following years. Making a huge tax provision for a lump sum payment that may become due several years hence is one way to take a big bath.

Big Board
The **NYSE**.

bite the bullet
Go ahead, **take the contra loss!** (See also **contra gain**.)

Black Monday
October 19, 1987. (See **Crash of October 1987**.)

Black Thursday
October 29, 1929. (See **Crash of October 1929**.)

block
Usually of shares. A large quantity that is part of a single transaction. (Sometimes incorrectly referred to as a 'bloc' which is a union or coalition of countries or parties with common social or political ideologies.)

Bloomberg
International wire service with excellent business and **investment** coverage.

BLR
base lending rate.

blue chip
A sterling, A-grade company or its stock. It usually takes a long time for any company to prove the consistent high quality of its products and its return on investment (**ROI**).

BNM
Bank Negara Malaysia.

board
See **board of directors**.

board lot
The generally accepted unit of share transactions. In countries such as Singapore and Malaysia, the typical board lot size is 1,000 shares, so if you choose to buy 'some' shares of ABC Ltd or DEF Bhd, the minimum number of shares you can buy *easily* at any one time is 1,000. In the US the usual board lot size is 100.

board of directors
Often simply referred to as the 'board'. These are people responsible for the overall running of a company. Generally there is a division between executive directors and non-executive directors. Executive directors are employed by the company to directly manage its affairs.

Non-executive ones play a more passive role and probably have other jobs outside the company. The **chairman** oversees the board, though the extent of his own role depends on whether he is an executive chairman. If he is a non-executive one, he often just plays the role of a figurehead, with the managing director truly calling the shots.

Bombay Sensitive Index
The 30-share **benchmark index** of India's most important bourse, the Bombay Stock Exchange.

bond

A long-term IOU issued by a company, municipality or even country. It has attached to it a **coupon rate** and a **maturity date**. Bond prices move in the opposite direction to interest rates. When interest rates fall bonds become more attractive and their prices tend to rise. Conversely when interest rates rise, bonds lose their allure since their fixed coupon rates then become less attractive than bank deposits. (See **coupon yield**.)

bonus issue

If a company has sufficient shareholders' funds built up from its retained earnings over the years, its board may choose to reward shareholders by issuing new shares. If a 1–for–2 bonus issue is declared, then a shareholder with 20,000 shares will end up with 10,000 more. Generally speaking though nothing has intrinsically changed with the company. Therefore, logically speaking the company's **market capitalisation** should not change. This means that the new equity base including the 50% increase in the number of shares should see a per share price adjustment. If previously the shares had been trading at $3, after the bonus issue they should trade at $\{2/(1 + 2)\} \times \$3 = \$2$.

As a general rule the expected adjustment in share price for an X–for–Y bonus issue, where X bonus shares are given out for every Y old shares held is:

Adjusted share price = {Y/(X+Y)} x the old price

In practice however because of the greater **liquidity** arising from more shares in the hands of investors and also because many companies prefer to maintain or even increase the dividend paid out on each share, there is usually a price adjustment to a level above the theoretically calculated price.

bookbuilding

As the term suggests it involves 'building a book'. This is done by a middleman who garners interest in an **asset** from various potential buyers and notes down how much of the asset each wants and at what price. The same is done for the sellers. The bookbuilder then can assess, based on **supply and demand**, a fair market price for this asset.

book (the seller)

Buy now – at whatever higher price the seller is offering. This is in direct contrast to **give (the buyer)**.

book value

The theoretical value of a company based on its **balance sheet**. This usually has no bearing on the company's market worth which is defined by its **market capitalisation**, as most of the time market capitalisation is a function of the company's expected **earnings per share** and the **P/E** multiple the market attaches to it.

book value per share

The **book value** of a company divided by the number of **share**s it has in its **equity base**.

boom

Attractive period of heightened economic activity. In Southeast Asia this has in recent years been predictably accompanied by hefty GDP growth rates, virtually zero unemployment levels and external confidence exhibited by large **FDI** inflows. While the **stock market** is generally viewed as a leading indicator of an economy's future fortunes, sometimes it is possible for equities to languish while the underlying economy chugs along healthily for years.

bottom fisher (trawler)

When markets fall, as they are wont to do, as in the case of the **Crash of October 1987**, it is normal for the stocks of sound companies to plummet along with those less sterling ones. When that happens a cash rich investor who selectively picks up what he considers bargains is engaged in bottom fishing or trawling.

bottom out
Much like the trajectory of an aeroplane that pulls out of a nose dive, the general market or even a particular investment can see periods of drops that eventually fade out. The investment is said to bottom out before staging a recovery.

bourse
A **stock exchange**. (Note the word rhymes with 'purse' and not with 'course'.)

boutique stocks
Similar to **illiquid stocks**. Just as boutique dress designs are less often seen on the street than those off-the-rack ones in department stores, boutique stocks derive their name from the relative rarity of finding these stocks traded.

"brain equity"
Using your head to study the ins and outs of **investments** so as to be rich enough to buy hundreds of copies of this book for all your friends.

breakout
It is quite common for a stock, or some other instrument, to trade for a long time within a tight price range. Then if something happens to alter its prospects, its price can either plummet or shoot up outside the previous range. This phenomenon is called the breakout.

Bretton Woods System
A **currency exchange rate** fixing mechanism put in place in 1947 by the **IMF**, which completely failed in 1973 in the wake of an explosion of US dollar liquidity in 1970 and 1971. (See **Triffin dilemma**.)

broker

The term originated with dealers in wine who would break open wine barrels in the course of their business. Today the term 'broker' refers to financial middlemen who act as intermediaries between buyers and sellers for a fee. (See **commission** and **disintermediation**.)

brokerage

Originally the fee charged for broking a deal, also **commission**. Today it refers primarily to stock broking firms, for example, **RHB**.

Buffett, Warren Edward

Born August 30, 1930, generally regarded as the greatest of investment guru Benjamin **Graham**'s disciples. When Buffett studied under Graham in Columbia in the 1950s he earned the only A+ the genius professor in investment ever gave in his (up to the point of Buffett's graduation) 22 years at the prestigious Manhattan-based university. Buffett is generally acclaimed as the world's most successful investor whose exploits are an embarrassment to adherents of the **Random Walk Theory**. His 47.5% of his listed vehicle **Berkshire Hathaway** is at the time of writing worth over US$18bn. His career in stocks began at the age of 11 when he bought three shares of a company called City Services. Berkshire, as Buffett always refers to his company, has significant stakes in numerous companies throughout America including household names like The Coca-Cola Company and The Washington Post Company.

In the words of Peter **Lynch**, from the foreword of Robert G. Hagstrom, Jr's book *The Warren Buffett Way – Investment Strategies of the World's Greatest Investor* (John Wiley & Sons, Inc., 1994):

> Warren Buffett is, first of all, very content. He loves everything he does, dealing with people and reading mass quantities of annual and quarterly reports and numerous newspapers and periodicals. As an investor he has discipline, patience, flexibility, courage, confidence, and decisiveness. He is always

searching for investments where risk is eliminated or minimised ...
Warren Buffett stresses that the critical investment factor is determining the intrinsic value of a business and paying a fair or bargain price. He doesn't care what the general **stock market** has done recently or will do in the future. (pp. iv and v)

(See also **Security Analysis** and **Graham, Benjamin.**)
(Note, 'Buffett' is pronounced the same way as a 'buffeting wind' and not as a 'buffet meal'.)

bull
An investor who thinks the **stock market** will head **north**.

bull market
A rising **stock market**, usually over a protracted period stretching many months or years.

bumiputras
The Malays and other indigenous peoples of Malaysia, accounting for slightly over half the 21m population.

buy
To purchase a **stock**, **bond** or any other **asset**. When an **investment analyst** makes a buy recommendation he expects the **investment** to outperform its **benchmark index**.

buy and hold
A **passive investment strategy** involving nothing more than purchasing an asset and sitting tight through several economic and market cycles. The aim is to make money on the general long-term trend of the asset's appreciation. The **stock market** is the greatest rewarder for long-term investors who buy, in the first place, sound companies, and then decide to ignore the short-term vagaries of the market. (See **Mr Market**.)

C

C
The single letter code for Chrysler, a company listed on the **NYSE**. (See **stock symbol**.)

CAGR
compound(ed) annual growth rate (depending on tense and usage).

call option
This instrument gives the holder a right to buy the **underlying investment** in question at a specified price within a set period, as opposed to a **put option** which affords the holder the right to sell that investment. (See **option**.)

call option holder
Owner of a **call option** who believes that the **underlying investment** will rise in price. (See **holder** and **put option holder**.)

capacity utilisation
The amount, in percentage terms, being used of a plant's ability to churn out goods. When analysing the performance of the overall manufacturing sector or of a particular industrial concern, scrutinising the capacity utilisation gives indications of how much more growth can be sustained without additional **capital expenditure**.

capex
capital expenditure.

capital
Any wealth employed or invested for the purpose of creating more of the same. (See **principal** and **profit**.)

Capital Adequacy Ratio
CAR. (See **Basle Accord**.)

capital allowances
Tax breaks for **capital expenditure** that are spread over many years, typically over the life of the **asset** used to generate wealth, like plant machinery and heavy vehicles.

Capital Asset Pricing Model
CAPM. (See **alpha**.)

capital expenditure
Money spent to purchase **capital goods**. Often abbreviated to '**capex**'.

capital gain
The gain resulting from the sale of **asset**s (= proceeds – original cost).

capital goods
Items bought by a business in the hope of using them to generate wealth. For a power company, generating plants would be capital goods, for an airline, aeroplanes. (See **depreciation**.)

capitalisation
Although it usually refers to the **common stock** issued by a company, in a broader sense it can also include all other securities issued by it including **preferred stock**, **bond**s and **debenture**s. (See **capital stock**.)

capital loss
The loss resulting from the sale of **assets** (= original cost – proceeds).

capital preservation
The first rule of **investment** is said by many (including **Buffett** and **Graham**) to merely be 'to not lose any money'. That encapsulates the philosophy behind capital preservation which maintains that once **capital** is lost, so too are the earnings that might have flowed from it. This does not preclude the taking on of **risk**, but rather warns against the excesses of greedy **speculation**. (See **Clason's Law 4** and **Clason's Law 5**.)

capital stock
All **common stock** plus all **preferred stock** of a company. (See **capitalisation**.)

CAPM
Capital Asset Pricing Model. (See **alpha**.)

CAR
Capital adequacy ratio. A yardstick of a bank's health and strength. Under the **Basle Accord** all banks should maintain a minimum CAR of 8%. The higher above this base-line a bank is, the more it can potentially lend out without requiring a **cash call** on its shareholders. Investors looking to buy healthy banks often look at the CAR to see if it is likely to fall below 8% in the near-term, thus necessitating a **cash call**.

cash
Generally hard **currency**, or real **money** as opposed to other **assets** in kind like **stocks**, **real estate** and **collectibles**. However, in the **futures** market, the term 'cash market' refers to the **equities** market because of the ease in which stocks may be sold for hard currency.

cash call
This is a call by the **board** for more capital funds to be injected into a company by **shareholders**. This is usually done by both listed and privately-held companies by way of a **rights issue**.

cash cow
In any **conglomerate** there will be some businesses that do better than others at any point in time. That one business that generates the most cash up front is deemed the cash cow that is often milked to fund expansion in other parts of the group.

cash dividend
A **dividend** paid in **cash**, as opposed to a **stock dividend**.

cash extraction
A fancy term used by **fund manager**s to denote the process of taking some **money** out of an **investment** that has appreciated. For instance, a British **fund manager** looks at a Malaysian investment, Banyak Bagus Bhd, which he had earlier bought at RM5 a **share** and that has doubled in price since then. He might then decide to sell his **stock** in the **company** and instead buy corresponding **warrants** to gain equivalent exposure to Banyak Bagus. If the shares are now trading at RM10, and the warrants at RM5, he can sell the shares, buy the warrants and extract cash from the investment which can then be redeployed in another company elsewhere in the region, say, Indonesia's equally hypothetical PT Lebih Banyak Bagus.

cash flow per share
Net cash flow (after taxes) derived for each year under scrutiny from a well-formulated **cash flow statement** divided by the **weighted average number of common shares** for the year in question. A consistently rising trend in cash flow per share generally augurs well for a company.

cash flow statement

A primary tool of any **financial analyst** building an earnings model of a company. The cash flow statement looks at **net profit** for any year and then adds back all non-cash subtractions, like depreciation, and subtracts items like **capital expenditure** and **dividend** payout which are not reflected in the original determination of net earnings.

If the final line item of a cash flow statement, namely the net cash movement for the year, is negative, this suggests that the company must go deeper into debt to finance that deficit or perhaps have a **cash call**. A company that consistently operates on a cash flow deficit basis is headed for trouble in the long-term. (See **net cash position** and **net change in cash**.)

cash per share

All the cash in a company's coffers divided by the number of shares outstanding.

CD

Certificate of deposit, another term for a fixed deposit account.

CDS

Central Depository System, Malaysia's scripless trading system that is gradually being implemented. It is not a completely scripless system, in that it does not do away with the **scrip** of a company. Rather it *immobilises* all scrip in a central depository area, and tracks ownership through an electronic system. A big advantage of the CDS is that it serves as an automatic mode of registering subsequent ownership of shares and entitlements (to **dividends** and **bonus issue**s and so on) that go with that original ownership stake.

central bank

The primary regulator of a nation's banking sector, like the **Bank of England** and **Bank Negara**.

Central Depository System
CDS.

Central Limit Order Book
CLOB.

CEO
chief executive officer.

CFA
Chartered Financial Analyst.

CFO
chief financial officer.

chairman
The person who chairs **board** meetings of a company. He is the highest ranked officer within the company though he may not have the most executive authority (that is usually reserved for the **CEO** or **MD**) unless he is executive chairman.

Chartered Financial Analyst
Highly coveted US-based programme of annual examinations customised to test the mettle of **investment analyst**s and their ilk over a three-year period. The holder of the qualification is entitled to put the highly coveted three letters, **CFA**, after his name. This qualification is generally deemed more valuable than an MBA (Master of Business Administration) for those in the **investment** business.

chartist
A **technical analyst**. (See **technical analysis**.)

chrometophobia
The fear of **money**. Not a widespread malady among **stock market** enthusiasts.

churning
Because **brokers** charge a **commission** on any trade done, some 'bad apples' in their midst have been known to constantly 'churn' a client's account to continually skim off commissions. To do this, such brokers often encourage gullible clients to overtrade. Eventually the client's account is either badly or wholly depleted.

Clason, George Samuel
The founder of the Clason Map Company of Denver, Colorado. He published the first road atlas of the United States and Canada. But Clason is most famous as the author of a series of 'Babylonian parables' he began issuing in 1926. These were later compiled into the financial inspirational classic, *The Richest Man in Babylon* (Penguin Books, 1988). To quote from Clason's foreword:

> Babylon became the wealthiest city of the ancient world because its citizens were the richest people of their time. They appreciated the value of money. They practised sound financial principles in acquiring money, keeping money and making their money earn more money. They provided for themselves what we all desire ... incomes for the future.

Leaving aside the fact that Babylon itself had no future, Clason's fictitious tales contain ageless truths revolving around thrift and sensible guidelines for investing. Some of these are crystallised in the **Seven Cures for a Lean Purse** and **Five Laws of Gold** which Clason has his 'richest man', **Arkad,** share generously with all who would listen to sound advice. (See Clason's **Law 1** to **Law 5** and **Arkad's Cure 1** to **7 for a Lean Purse.**)

Clason's Law 1
Gold cometh gladly and in increasing quantity to any man who will put by not less than one-tenth of his earnings to create an estate for his future and that of his family.

Clason's Law 2
Gold laboureth diligently and contentedly for the wise owner who finds for it profitable employment, multiplying even as the flocks of the field.

Clason's Law 3
Gold clingeth to the protection of the cautious owner who invests it under the advice of men wise in its handling.

Clason's Law 4
Gold slippeth away from the man who invests it in businesses or purposes with which he is not familiar or which are not approved by those skilled in its keep.

Clason's Law 5
Gold flees the man who would force it to impossible earnings or who followeth the alluring advice of tricksters and schemers or who trusts it to his own inexperience and romantic desires in investment.

Class A
Chinese shares officially reserved for domestic investors to protect China's **forex** reserves. (See **Shanghai A Share** and **Shenzen A Share**.)

Class B
Chinese shares set aside for foreigners to invest in. (See **Shanghai B Share** and **Shenzen B Share**.)

class of options
Options of the same class are of the same type, either **call** or **put** options, and cover the same **underlying investment**.

CLOB
Central Limit Order Book, an **OTC market** of primarily Malaysian stocks in Singapore.

closed-end fund

Also called an investment trust or investment company in the UK. In terms of getting funds from fresh subscribers, it is a **mutual fund** that raises money only once through a direct issue of shares or units in the fund. However, even a closed-end fund can raise more money if it so chooses through, for instance, a **rights issue**. If a closed-end fund is also traded on an exchange, it is also referred to as an **exchange-traded fund**. Because of this, the price of a closed-end fund unit fluctuates much like the price of a typical stock. Its price will move on the back of a complex interplay between investor demand (or lack of it) and the **NAV** of its **portfolio**. Some examples of closed-end funds are **APB, FPF, IGF, IF, JGF, KF, MF, SAF, SGF, TWN, TEMF, TC** and **TTF**. (See **open-end fund**.)

closing price

the price at which the final trade of an **investment** in any one trading session is transacted.

closing purchase

In options trading, this refers to the purchase of an **option** at precisely the same terms as one originally sold. This balancing exercise wipes the books clean and liquidates the **writer**'s position and obligation.

closing sale

In options trading, this refers to the sale of an **option** at precisely the same terms as one originally bought. This balancing exercise wipes the books clean and liquidates the **holder**'s position (but not his obligation since there never was one to start off with, see **put option**).

closing transaction

The very last trade done during a single session of a **market**.

Code of Ethics

A stringent set of ethical guidelines **financial analyst**s affiliated to the US-based Association for Investment Management and Research

(AIMR) all over the world are expected to comply with. The Code is issued by the AIMR. A recent version is replicated below:

> A financial analyst should conduct himself with integrity and dignity and act in an ethical manner in his dealings with the public, clients, customers, employers, employees and fellow analysts.
>
> A financial analyst should conduct himself and should encourage others to practice financial analysis in a professional and ethical manner that will reflect credit on himself and his profession.
>
> A financial analyst should act with competence and should strive to maintain and improve his competence and that of others in the profession.
>
> A financial analyst should use proper care and exercise independent professional judgment.

(Haim Levy, *Introduction to Investments*, South-Western College Publishing, 1996, Appendix 2)

collectibles

Any items at all that serve as alternative **investments** to the more conventional **stock**s, **bond**s, derivatives and real estate. The name is derived from the involvement of a collector who usually builds a collection of coins, comics, gems, gold rings, paintings, rugs or anything else, out of a sheer love for them and not primarily for **capital gain**.

commission

What **broker**s live for; also called **brokerage** charges. In both Malaysia and Singapore, for instance, different graduated scales exist for the determination of commissions payable on each transaction. Generally, commission rates fall as the size of the transaction rises. For small deals where the 1% ceiling rate is charged, a purchase of 1 **lot** of Alpha Bhd at $2 a share will result in a commission charge of $20. If the stock is then sold at $2.10, another $21 will be charged by the broker in commission. The investor's net position then (ignoring stamp duties) is worked out by looking at his outlay of $(2 x 1000 + 20) = $2020; and his return of $(2.1 x 1000 − 21) = $2079. In this transaction he would have made $59.

common equity
common stock.

common shares
common stock or ordinary shares.

common stock
Pieces of paper or their electronic equivalents which denote proportional ownership of a company. For instance, in Malaysia, Tenaga Nasional has a paid up capital of about RM3bn denominated in 3bn shares with a **nominal value** of RM1. If an **investor** owns 30 **lot**s of Tenaga, that amounts to 30,000 shares − his common stock holding in the company. He literally owns 30,000/3,000,000,000 or 1/100,000th of the company. (See **share**.)

Common Stocks and Uncommon Profits
The most famous book of modern investment theory pioneer Philip A. **Fisher**. The most useful portions of the book revolve around **Fisher's 15 Points** to look for in companies worth buying.

company
A business organisation that is set up, quite literally incorporated, as a legal entity separate from its shareholders. Each company has its functions demarcated by its **articles of association** and **memorandum of association**.

Composite Index, CI
Like the **dollar** for currencies, the Composite Index is the most common name for a stock exchange index. A partial list follows of the **bourse**s that call at least one of their major indices, the CI:

Jakarta Stock Exchange, Kuala Lumpur Stock Exchange, Manila Stock Exchange and the Seoul Stock Exchange.

compound(ed) annual growth rate

Usually abbreviated to **CAGR**. The average growth each year a company has seen over a period of several years, on a compounded basis. For example, if we examine the turnover of company LMN Ltd from Year 0 to Year 3 we might find that it shrunk from $10m to $9m, then grew to $15m, and then grew some more to $20m. The CAGR in this case over the three-year period in question is 24%. This is easily understood if you consider the **Year-on-Year** growth rate, first. Between Year 0 and Year 1, turnover contracted by 10% or if you prefer grew by −10%. Between Year 1 and Year 2 it jumped 67%. It then grew 33% to finish off at **$20m**. Looking at a series of growth rates like: −10%, +67%, +33%, is a little mind-numbing. It is easier to get a handle on the long-term improvement of the company by considering its CAGR. This is worked out by taking revenue for Year 3 and looking at the improvement over revenue for Year 0. In this case it is $10m ($20m − $10m), or in percentage terms the jump over that period has been 100%. Applying the following formula over the period:

CAGR = {[(Revenue in Year N)/(Revenue in Year 0)]$^{1/N}$− 1} × 100%
= {[20m/10m]$^{1/3}$ − 1} × 100%
= 26%.

This means that if you average out the growth on a year to year basis and assume a steady 26% growth rate you will end up with the same result at the end of Year 3.

Consider this averaged out series showing a steady 26% annual growth: Year 0 = $10m, Year 1 = $12.6m, Year 2 = $15.9m, and finally Year 3 = **$20m**.

For those who are averse to using a complex CAGR formula, in some circumstances the use of the Rule of 72 makes for rapid approximate calculations. (See **Rule of 72**.) In this present example, with turnover doubling from $10m to $20m, in 3 years, taking 72 and dividing it by 3 gives 24%, which is fairly close to the 26% we worked out using the precise CAGR formula.

compounding

The effect of **compound interest**. Most rewarding when applied to the **stock market** which has historically outperformed every other form of **investment** in the long run.

It is empirically proven that *consistently* timing the market, as in always determining exactly when the market is at a peak and when it is at a trough, is virtually impossible. Because of this fact and through the pleasant ministrations of compounding, investment research over many decades suggests that being **fully invested** at all times is the most consistent way to grow wealthy.

compound interest

The magical phenomenon similar to snowballing that makes long-term investing a relatively low risk activity. Interest earned in one period becomes part of the principal amount in the next period and begins to earn interest on itself. (See **simple interest** and **compounded annual growth rate**.)

conglomerate

Large corporate group containing many companies, be they subsidiaries or associates or a mix of these, that are involved in a range of businesses.

consideration

In accounting terms, this refers to the compensation given in return for some benefit. If a man buys a house, he gives money in consideration of that deal.

constant dollar plan

A method of investing equal amounts of money at regular intervals. The advantage of such a plan is that in times of high prices fewer units of the investment are bought and in times of low prices, more units are bought. This has the pleasant effect of ironing out **market timing** errors, since you're always buying regardless of how **Mr Market** is acting. This sort of plan brings the average cost of acquisition well below the all-time highs. This process is called **dollar-cost averaging**.

contra
Potentially risky method of speculating by buying or selling **stock** and effecting a corresponding transaction within the period stipulated by the exchange for settlement – be it by a cash payment or a **scrip** delivery. (See **contra gain** and **contra loss**.)

contra gain
Money made on a **contra** play.

contra loss
Money lost on a **contra** play. Sadly, far more common than a **contra gain** since the typical contra player lacks the holding power to give him an edge over the short-term vagaries of the **market**.

contrarian
One who buys when all others are selling, and sells when all others are buying. The most famous contrarian investor of all time was Baron Rothschild who is said to have claimed, "Buy when there is blood on the streets."

contrarian investing
The investment strategy of a **contrarian**.

convertible bond
A long-term debt security that has the **option** to be converted into **common stock** through an additional payment and within a set time. (See **capitalisation**.)

corporate bond
A long-term **IOU** or bond issued by a corporation to retire more expensive loans, to raise **capital** for expansion, to increase **working capital** or to finance **takeover**s.

corporate insiders
High ranking people within a company's hierarchy, certainly including its **board**, who are privy to **inside information**.

counter
listed company.

coupon
A **bond** interest payment. (See **coupon rate**.)

coupon rate
The interest rate on a **bond**, stated as a percentage of the **nominal value**. For instance, if the coupon rate of a bond is 5%, and if the nominal value of the bond is $1, the issuer of the bond will pay the owner of the bond 5 cents every year for the life of that long-term loan instrument. (See **junk bond**.)

coupon yield
Coupon rate divided by the current **bond** price, denoted in percentage terms. For instance if a bond has a stated coupon rate of 10% and if its nominal value is $1, it pays 10 cents on that bond each year. If at a time of low interest rates the bond is trading at $1.50, the current coupon yield is $= (10/150 \times 100\%) = 6.67\%$.

If however at a time of high interest rates when bank deposits are typically paying 12% perhaps, there is no logical reason to want to hold on to a bond that only has a coupon yield of 6.67%. As bond holders start selling the bond, its price should fall to $0.83. It is likely to stay at that level for a while since its coupon yield has now risen to 12%. This is easily worked out:

$$(10/83) \times 100\% = 12\%$$

This explains why bond prices and interest rates move in opposite directions.

CPA
Certified Public Accountant.

CPF
Singapore's Central Provident Fund. (Also see **EPF**.)

CPI
Consumer Price Index. The primary **inflation** indicator of many countries.

CPO
crude palm oil.

Crash of October 1929
Happened on **Black Thursday**, October 29, 1929, when the crash of the **NYSE** precipitated the **Great Depression**. Although the DJIA fell 12.8%, the crash of 58 years later was worse in market terms but much easier on the general economy. (See **Crash of October 1987**.) An interesting footnote of history is that in the aftermath of that crash Richard Whitney, president of the **NYSE** was thrown in prison for fraud.

Crash of October 1987
A relatively recent drop in global equities precipitated by another crash of the **NYSE** on **Black Monday**, October 1987, that did not act as a precursor of bad times but was rather a glitch exacerbated by programmed selling. This is despite the DJIA falling 22.6%, almost twice as steep a fall in overall terms as the **Crash of October 1929**. (See **October** and **NYSE**.)

credit risk

A form of **risk** every lender and even **investor** faces exposure to – that the business will not be able to generate returns to pay interest or dividends.

cross rates

All other **currencies** are primarily quoted in the world market against the de facto global currency, the US dollar. It is therefore possible to use two of these primary benchmark figures to determine the rate of currency A against currency B – where neither is the US dollar. This new figure would be the cross rate of the two currencies. (See **currencies**.)

The forex rates table on pages 52–53 shows the cross rates of 23 different currencies against each other calculated using their primary exchange rate against the US dollar. (Rates of August 23, 1996, as quoted in the **AWSJ** of August 26, 1996. Because rates are constantly in a state of flux, this example only serves as an indication of what relative rates were like in the third quarter of 1996.) The first line of the table shows the official exchange rate of the various currencies against the US dollar. For instance, 2300 Riel (the Cambodian currency) is equivalent to US$1, while NZ$1.44 = US$1. It is therefore relatively easy to figure out that 2300 Riel = NZ$1.44, and to then calculate the **cross rate** of 1592 Riel = NZ$1. Looked at another way, 1 Riel = NZ$0.0006. The cross rates in this example help Kiwi travellers to Cambodia figure out just how rich they are there, while Cambodian visitors to New Zealand will probably think twice before buying even a single sheepskin rug. (See **exchange rate**.)

cross trade

A securities transaction where the same dealer brokers both the buy and sell side of a deal. This is particularly lucrative as double the usual commission can be earned, although it is common practice for cross trades on large blocks of shares to be done on reduced broking commissions.

Forex Rates

	US $	A $	Taka	B $	Kyat	Riel
USA	**1.0000**	**1.26**	**42.31**	**1.41**	**5.86**	**2300.00**
Australia	0.7943	1.0000	33.6072	1.1209	4.6508	1826.8467
Bangladesh	0.0236	0.0298	1.0000	0.0334	0.1384	54.3587
Brunei	0.7086	0.8921	29.9826	1.0000	4.1492	1629.8186
Myanmar(Burma)	0.1708	0.2150	7.2262	0.2410	1.0000	392.8065
Cambodia	0.0004	0.0005	0.0184	0.0006	0.0025	1.0000
China	0.1204	0.1516	5.0934	0.1699	0.7049	276.8716
Hong Kong	0.1293	0.1628	5.4711	0.1825	0.7571	297.3997
India	0.0280	0.0353	1.1854	0.0395	0.1640	64.4348
Indonesia	0.0004	0.0005	0.0181	0.0006	0.0025	0.9826
Japan	0.0092	0.0116	0.3905	0.0130	0.0540	21.2246
North Korea	0.4651	0.5856	19.6798	0.6564	2.7234	1069.7674
South Korea	0.0012	0.0015	0.0517	0.0017	0.0072	2.8093
Laos	0.0011	0.0014	0.0460	0.0015	0.0064	2.5000
Macao	0.1252	0.1576	5.2963	0.1766	0.7329	287.8995
Malaysia	0.4010	0.5049	16.9680	0.5659	2.3481	922.3612
New Zealand	0.6923	0.8716	29.2935	0.9770	4.0538	**1592.36**
Pakistan	0.0281	0.0353	1.1879	0.0396	0.1644	64.5725
Philippines	0.0381	0.0480	1.6140	0.0538	0.2234	87.7360
Singapore	0.7086	0.8921	29.9826	1.0000	4.1492	1629.8186
Taiwan	0.0367	0.0462	1.5533	0.0518	0.2150	84.4347
Thailand	0.0395	0.0498	1.6720	0.0558	0.2314	90.8857
UK	1.5525	1.9546	65.6886	2.1909	9.0904	3570.7500
Vietnam	0.0000	0.0001	0.0039	0.0001	0.0005	0.2097

	SK Won	Kip	Pataca	Ringgit	NZ$	P Rupee
USA	**818.70**	**920.00**	**7.99**	**2.49**	**1.44**	**35.62**
Australia	650.2780	730.7387	6.3454	1.9806	1.1473	28.2914
Bangladesh	19.3493	21.7435	0.1888	0.0589	0.0341	0.8418
Brunei	580.1446	651.9274	5.6611	1.7670	1.0235	25.2402
Myanmar (Burma)	139.8220	157.1226	1.3644	0.4259	0.2467	6.0832
Cambodia	0.3560	0.4000	0.0035	0.0011	**0.0006**	0.0155
China	98.5542	110.7486	0.9617	0.3002	0.1739	4.2878
Hong Kong	105.8614	118.9599	1.0330	0.3224	0.1868	4.6057
India	22.9360	25.7739	0.2238	0.0699	0.0405	0.9979
Indonesia	0.3498	0.3930	0.0034	0.0011	0.0006	0.0152
Japan	7.5550	8.4898	0.0737	0.0230	0.0133	0.3287
North Korea	380.7907	427.9070	3.7158	1.1598	0.6718	16.5669
South Korea	1.0000	1.1237	0.0098	0.0030	0.0018	0.0435
Laos	0.8899	1.0000	0.0087	0.0027	0.0016	0.0387
Macao	102.4797	115.1598	1.0000	0.3121	0.1808	4.4585
Malaysia	328.3205	368.9445	3.2038	1.0000	0.5792	14.2841
New Zealand	566.8097	636.9427	5.5309	1.7264	24.6600	18.1494
Pakistan	22.9850	25.8290	0.2243	0.0700	0.0406	1.0000
Philippines	31.2302	35.0944	0.3047	0.0951	0.0551	1.3587
Singapore	580.1446	651.9274	5.6611	1.7670	1.0235	25.2402
Taiwan	30.0551	33.7739	0.2933	0.0915	0.0530	1.3076
Thailand	32.3514	36.3543	0.3157	0.0985	0.0571	1.4075
UK	1271.0318	1428.3000	12.4028	3.8713	2.2424	55.2983
Vietnam	0.0746	0.0839	0.0007	0.0002	0.0001	0.0032

Forex Rates

	Renminbi/Yuan	HK$	I Rupee	Rupiah	Yen	NK Won
USA	8.31	7.73	35.70	2340.70	108.37	2.15
Australia	6.5982	6.1427	28.3519	1859.1739	86.0723	1.7077
Bangladesh	0.1963	0.1828	0.8436	55.3207	2.5611	0.0508
Brunei	5.8866	5.4802	25.2941	1658.6593	76.7893	1.5235
Myanmar (Burma)	1.4187	1.3208	6.0962	399.7575	18.5072	0.3672
Cambodia	0.0036	0.0034	0.0155	1.0177	0.0471	0.0009
China	1.0000	0.9310	4.2969	281.7710	13.0449	0.2588
Hong Kong	1.0741	1.0000	4.6155	302.6624	14.0121	0.2780
India	0.2327	0.2167	1.0000	65.5750	3.0359	0.0602
Indonesia	0.0035	0.0033	0.0152	1.0000	0.0463	0.0009
Japan	0.0767	0.0714	0.3294	21.6001	1.0000	0.0198
North Korea	3.8638	3.5971	16.6023	1088.6977	50.4023	1.0000
South Korea	0.0101	0.0094	0.0436	2.8590	0.1324	0.0026
Laos	0.0090	0.0084	0.0388	2.5442	0.1178	0.0023
Macao	1.0398	0.9681	4.4681	292.9940	13.5644	0.2691
Malaysia	3.3314	3.1014	14.3146	938.6830	43.4573	0.8622
New Zealand	5.7512	5.3543	24.7127	1620.5345	75.0242	1.4885
Pakistan	0.2332	0.2171	1.0021	65.7151	3.0423	0.0604
Philippines	0.3169	0.2950	1.3616	89.2886	4.1337	0.0820
Singapore	5.8866	5.4802	25.2941	1658.6593	76.7893	1.5235
Taiwan	0.3050	0.2839	1.3104	85.9288	3.9782	0.0789
Thailand	0.3283	0.3056	1.4105	92.4940	4.2821	0.0850
UK	12.8968	12.0066	55.4165	3633.9368	168.2367	3.3379
Vietnam	0.0008	0.0007	0.0033	0.2134	0.0099	0.0002

	Peso	S$	NT $	Baht	Pound	Dong
USA	26.22	1.41	27.24	25.31	0.64	10970.00
Australia	20.8221	1.1209	21.6362	20.1005	0.5116	8713.2645
Bangladesh	0.6196	0.0334	0.6438	0.5981	0.0152	259.2676
Brunei	18.5764	1.0000	19.3027	17.9326	0.4564	7773.5261
Myanmar (Burma)	4.4771	0.2410	4.6522	4.3220	0.1100	1873.5163
Cambodia	0.0114	0.0006	0.0118	0.0110	0.0003	4.7696
China	3.1557	0.1699	3.2791	3.0464	0.0775	1320.5571
Hong Kong	3.3897	0.1825	3.5222	3.2722	0.0833	1418.4672
India	0.7344	0.0395	0.7631	0.7090	0.0180	307.3260
Indonesia	0.0112	0.0006	0.0116	0.0108	0.0003	4.6866
Japan	0.2419	0.0130	0.2514	0.2335	0.0059	101.2319
North Korea	12.1930	0.6564	12.6698	11.7705	0.2996	5102.3256
South Korea	0.0320	0.0017	0.0333	0.0309	0.0008	13.3993
Laos	0.0285	0.0015	0.0296	0.0275	0.0007	11.9239
Macao	3.2814	0.1766	3.4097	3.1677	0.0806	1373.1553
Malaysia	10.5129	0.5659	10.9240	10.1486	0.2583	4399.2621
New Zealand	18.1494	0.9770	18.8590	17.5204	0.4459	7594.8491
Pakistan	0.7360	0.0396	0.7648	0.7105	0.0181	307.9826
Philippines	1.0000	0.0538	1.0391	0.9653	0.0246	418.4627
Singapore	18.5764	1.0000	19.3027	17.9326	0.4564	7773.5261
Taiwan	0.9624	0.0518	1.0000	0.9290	0.0236	402.7166
Thailand	1.0359	0.0558	1.0764	1.0000	0.0255	433.4855
UK	40.6988	2.1909	42.2901	39.2883	1.0000	17030.9250
Vietnam	0.0024	0.0001	0.0025	0.0023	0.0000	1.0000

CULS
Convertible unsecured loan stock.

cum
'With' as opposed to **ex**, which means 'without'. For instance, if a stock is bought cum dividend, this means it is bought before the **ex dividend date** for that entitlement, and the buyer will qualify for the **dividend**. If you bought 1,000 shares of EFG Ltd cum dividend, you qualify for the dividends attached to those shares. If you paid $2.15 for each share, and if a $0.20 dividend (after tax) is soon to be paid on them, essentially you are only paying $1.95 for each share because you will very quickly have $0.20 a share, or $200, winging its way to you by way of a dividend cheque. Once the ex-date arrives, the **market** will immediately compensate for the loss of entitlement of the dividend (because the shares are now no longer trading cum dividend) and the price will fall $0.20. It would now be trading ex dividend, at a lower price due to the loss of entitlement.

currency
money.

currencies
The legal tender of various countries. Most sovereign nations have their own currencies that usually fall in one of three categories, a **free-floating exchange rate regime**, **pegged exchange rate regime** and a **managed floating exchange rate regime**. (Also see **cross rates**.)

currency, free float
currency of a nation that adopts a **free-floating exchange rate regime**.

currency, managed float
currency of a nation that adopts a **managed floating exchange rate regime**.

currency, pegged
currency of a nation that adopts a **pegged exchange rate regime**.

current account balance
A country's net income derived by subtracting its import costs from its export revenue. These take into account trade in both goods and services. While running a deficit here is generally deemed bad for a country's economy, close scrutiny should be paid to the reason for that situation. In the recently damaging case of Mexico in 1994 (for a brief discussion of Mexico's earlier 1982 currency debacle see **pegged exchange rate regime**), much of the deficit was funded by short term funds brought in for speculative purposes. When these took rapid flight, the peso took a horrendous beating. In the case of a country like Malaysia, however, the deficit is brought about by expensive, lumpy imports of capital and intermediate goods which will be used in the future to generate wealth for the nation. The deficit here (RM18.7bn in 1995, improving to RM13.0bn in 1996) is funded by long-term capital inflows, a markedly different situation. When assessing the viability of equity investments in a country, attention should be paid to the underlying reasons for a current account trade deficit, or even surplus.

current assets
All assets that can readily be converted into cash within one financial year. These include **cash**, **securities**, accounts receivable that reflect the trade debtors' position after factoring out the possibility of bad debts, and **inventory**. (See **working capital**, **current liabilities** and **net current assets**.)

current assets per share
current assets/number of **common shares** outstanding.

current liabilities
All debt and other payments due (like accounts payable that reflect the trade creditors' position) within one financial year. (See **working capital**, **current assets** and **net current assets**.)

current market value
The price of an **investment** being offered right now by **Mr Market**.

D

D
The single letter code for Dominion Resources, a company listed on the **NYSE**. (See **stock symbol**.)

DBS 50
Development Bank of Singapore 50, a secondary index of the **SES**. (See also **STII**.)

DCF
This often encountered abbreviation stands for discounted cash flow. It is a key concept in finance and investing and many **asset** valuation models are rooted in the DCF principle which simply states that the **present value** of an asset is the present value of all its future cash flows.

Therefore, this DCF concept is inextricably linked with the **time value of money**. Once you understand the principle underlying DCF analysis, you have a remarkably powerful valuation tool in your brain. At its most basic level, any valuation becomes a case of projecting all future cash flows and determining a fair discount rate to use on these cash flows to see what they are worth today. Admittedly, both the task of correctly projecting cash flows in the future and determining an appropriate discount rate are jobs that separate the men from the boys in any investment analysis arena.

But for the sake of our discussion, let us simply assume that if an asset costs $10 today and promises to pay you $12 next year and then immediately becomes worthless, if you choose to use a 10% discount rate, that single $12 payment would be worth $10.91 (= $12/(1 + 0.1) today. Since it costs only $10 to buy this future income injection of $12 one year from now (which is worth $10.91 in today's currency), it would appear a good buy. (See also examples given under the **present value**, **future value** and **time value of money** entries.)

dead duck
An **investor** or more likely **speculator** who is badly caught in a **bear trap**.

dealer
A **broker** of **stock**s, **bond**s, and derivatives who may earn a **commission** on deals done through him, but who also earns a salary paid by the **brokerage** he works for.

debenture
This is an interesting term for a specific species of **bond**. In the Asian region a debenture is a bond that is secured to a specific **asset** of a company, like a warehouse or certain items of factory equipment.

However in the US, it is an unsecured bond backed by the general (not specific, as in the Asian case) credit of the company.

debt
Money owed.

debt securities
IOUs like **bond**s that are traded in the open **market**.

defensive stock
A stock with a **beta** less than 1.0. (See **aggressive stock**.)

demand and supply
The basic economic forces that determine the price of an item in a free market. (See **market forces** and **analyst**.)

depreciation
The **currency** amount written off each year in a company's accounts to roughly compensate for the drop in value of **capital goods**. This money set aside is meant to fund the replacement of these goods, but is generally insufficient due to the effects of inflation. (See **straight line depreciation**.)

depression
A deep, abiding **recession** such as the Great Depression of the 1930s. Due to its protracted nature it is usually accompanied by long periods of lost confidence in the **stock market**. While some optimists may realise that underlying stocks are trading extremely cheaply by historical standards, there is precious little money around for a **bottom trawler** to take advantage of these bargain basement prices.

devaluation
A large drop in the value of a country's **currency**, relative to other currencies (see **cross rates** and **exchange rate**) brought about by economic collapse or an intentional move by its government to increase its export competitiveness.

dilution
In the investment context dilution refers to a thinning out, usually of either earnings or ownership.

Earnings dilution takes place, for instance, when a company doubles its share base to acquire another business that only increases its total earnings by 50%. If previously there were 1m shares with earnings of $1m, that works out to an **EPS** of $1. Now, if the new equation sees 2m shares with total earnings of only $1.5m, EPS now falls to 75 cents. The earnings per share dilution in this instance is 25%.

Ownership dilution takes place when an investor decides not to participate in a **rights** issue and sees his slice of the **equity** pie fall. In the case of a 1–for–2 rights issue at $4 a share, say a shareholder of a company with 2m paid up shares owns 2,000 shares. He therefore owns a one-thousandth interest in the company.

Because of his investment he gains the right to apply for another 1,000 shares at $4 a share. He may however decide that his car needs a major overhaul and he cannot afford to stump out $4,000 just then. In forgoing his right to the rights shares, his proportional ownership in the company falls. After the rights exercise is completed, he is left with his 2,000 original shares while the company's **equity base** has jumped from 2m to 3m shares. Our automotively challenged investor now owns 1 part in 1,500 of the company, no longer 1 part in 1,000. His ownership level has been diluted through his own inaction.

direct investment
Money that flows directly to a particular project instead of through an indirect investment in the **stock market**. (See **FDI**.)

direct listing
The listing of a company on the basis of its own track record and not through the backdoor machinations of a **takeover**.

discount
The amount, either in monetary or percentage terms, that a **stock** or **bond** trades at below a set mark. That mark can be its initial issue price, the market average **P/E** or even an industry average **P/E**. (See **premium** and **ELSOS**.)

discount house
A company that specialises in short-term money market operations. As its name suggests, a discount house, unlike a **money broker** which only makes money from fixed **commission**s, earns its income from the **spread** it gets on short-term paper. This would include

government paper, **BA**s and private debt securities. It buys these short-term instruments at a **discount** to their **face value**s and usually redeems them at the face values on maturity. Alternatively, a discount house could sell its paper to other parties, including other discount houses and enter into a repo, or repurchase agreement, to buy back the paper at a later stage. The traditional lines demarcating the functions of a discount house with those of merchant banks are now blurring. In some countries, including Singapore, the discount house has already gone the way of the dodo.

discretionary account
A brokerage account where the holder gives some level of autonomy to either his broker or fund manager to act on his behalf.

disintermediation
A fancy word that, when scrutinised, yields its meaning. It essentially involves buyers and sellers dealing directly with each other, cutting out the middle man or **broker**. (See **markets** and **money broker**.)

diversification
The act of not putting all your eggs in one basket. In investment terms this translates into spreading your investment dollars between different classes of investment like **common stock**s, **bond**s, **real estate** and **collectibles**. Also, within each class of investment spreading your largess around to different specific investments makes for good insurance against the vagaries of economics that may strike any industry at any time. (See **diversification risk**, **portfolio** and **Rainbow Effect**.)

diversification risk
A form of **risk** that arises either from too much or too little **diversification** of your **portfolio**. If there is too much diversification, the star performers in your basket of goodies cannot do much for the overall portfolio because the **capital gain** from them is masked by

poorer performers. And if there is too little diversification, the benefits of spreading your assets around are not fully realised with too much risk being taken on.

dividend

A payment in cash, or less commonly in **stock**, made from the **earnings** of a **company** to reward **shareholders**. For instance, if Cash Bulge Ltd made 40 cents in **EPS** for the last financial year, its board may choose to give 10 cents (gross rate) back to shareholders and retain 30 cents for its business expansion. (See **dividend cover**, **cash dividend** and **stock dividend**.)

For most long-term **stock market** investors the cumulative effect of annual dividends is a major plus factor in their investment strategy. This is especially true if the bulk of the net dividend income is reinvested wisely.

dividend cover

The number of times a company's earnings for the year can 'cover' its total dividend payments for that year. For instance, in the case of Cash Bulge Ltd (see **dividend**), if the effective corporate tax rate is 30%, when the company chooses to give 10 cents per share (from an **EPS** of 40 cents) back to its shareholders on a gross basis, what the happy shareholder ends up with in his pocket is 7 cents. The net dividend cover therefore is $40/7 = 5.7$ times. (See **gross dividend cover** and **payout ratio**.)

dividend per share

Commonly denoted as **DPS**. This can be expressed as either the net or gross dividend per share depending on whether taxes are factored out or not. In terms of real benefit to the shareholder, net dividend per share has greater relevance to personal enrichment.

The calculation is simple. Take in all dividends paid out over the year, usually interim plus final dividend declared, and divide by the weighted number of common shares for the year.

dividend reinvestment plan
Commonly called a **DRIP**. This is a special plan offered by some companies that pay their dividends as **stock dividend**s, not **cash dividend**s. This means that each time a stock dividend is declared a shareholder gets more shares in the company. However, it is worth noting that his proportional ownership in the company is unchanged – if he keeps all his stock dividends – as the company's **paid up capital** will rise in the same proportion as his number of shares. A big advantage of a DRIP is that it allows long-term investors the chance to invest in a company without paying a **commission** to a **dealer**.

dividend yield
Dividend amount as a percentage of the **stock**'s price. (See **yield**.)

DJIA
The **Dow Jones Industrial Average**.

dog
As a canine pet this can be man's best friend. But when it is used to describe a stock beware of portfolio rabies and don't buy it. (See **Greater Fool Theory**.)

dollar
Although it generally refers to the US dollar which is Planet Earth's de facto global currency (also known informally as the **greenback**), the dollar, like the **Composite Index** for stock indices, is the most common name for a currency with at least 37 countries adopting it for all or part of their currency's name.

 A partial list follows of the countries that call their currencies the dollar: Australia, Bahamas, Barbados, Belize, Bermuda, Brunei, Canada, Cayman Islands, Fiji, Guam, Guyana, Hong Kong, Jamaica, Kiribati, Liberia, Marshall Islands, Micronesia, Nauru, New Zealand, Palau, Pitcairn Island, Puerto Rico, St. Kitts and Nevis, St. Lucia, St. Vincent and the Grenadines, American Samoa, Singapore,

Solomon Islands, Taiwan, Tonga, Trinidad & Tobago, Turks & Caicos, Tuvalu, British Virgin Islands, US Virgin Islands, the USA and Zimbabwe. (Also see **currencies**.)

dollar-cost averaging
The process of applying a **constant dollar plan**.

Dong
The Vietnamese currency. (See **currencies**.)

double bottom
A price chart formation resembling an upper case 'W'. (See **W-formation**.)

double top
A price chart formation resembling an upper case 'M'. (See **M-formation**.)

Dow, Charles H.
The founder of the Dow-Jones financial news service which today owns the **Wall Street Journal** and its offshoots like the **Asian Wall Street Journal**. Charles Dow originally formulated the **Dow Jones Industrial Index** in 1884 and finally published his list in 1896 after 12 years of tinkering. Only General Electric survives till today from that original 1896 list. Dow's writings formed the core of the **Dow Theory** which is a touchstone for **technical analysis** today. His work has been expanded upon by technical practitioners like John **Magee** and Robert D. **Edwards**.

Dow Jones China 88
One of seven commonly quoted Chinese indices. (See also **Dow Jones Shanghai**, **Dow Jones Shenzen**, **Shanghai A Share**, **Shanghai B Share**, **Shenzen A Share** and **Shenzen B Share**.)

Dow Jones Industrial Average

The most closely followed **index** of the **NYSE**. Therefore this 30-stock index is the most closely followed stock index in the world. However, although to the man-on-the-street the **DJIA** is the benchmark index of the entire equities scene, the 30 component stocks only make up about a quarter of the NYSE's total market capitalisation. It is therefore deemed too unrepresentative to be the **benchmark index** for big US **institutional investors** who look instead to the **S&P 500**.

The DJIA was first formulated by Charles Dow in 1884 (with just 11 stocks) and after a dozen years of tinkering he first published it in 1896. Occasional changes are made to the composition of the list and on October 1, 1928, the list grew to its present size of 30. Below is the current rendering of the DJIA's component stocks:

1. AlliedSignal
2. ALCOA
   (Aluminium Company of America)
3. American Express
4. AT&T
5. Boeing
6. Caterpillar
7. Chevron
8. Coca-Cola
9. Disney
10. Du Pont
11. Eastman Kodak
12. Exxon
13. General Electric
14. General Motors
15. Goodyear
16. Hewlett-Packard Co
17. IBM
18. International Paper
19. Johnson & Johnson
20. McDonald's
21. Merck
22. JP Morgan
23. Philip Morris
24. Procter & Gamble
25. Sears
26. 3M
27. Travelers Group
28. Union Carbide
29. United Technologies
30. Wal-Mart Stores

(The Dow 30 as at March 17, 1997)

(For those interested in trivia, only one of the 30 companies above has survived the century-plus of winnowing and been on the list since Charles Dow first published his DJIA in 1896. The answer is found under the **Dow, Charles H.** entry.)

Dow Jones (HK) Small Cap
A secondary index of the **Hong Kong Stock Exchange**. (See also **Hang Seng Index** and **All Ordinaries**.)

Dow Jones Shanghai
An index of the **Shanghai Securities Exchange**. (See also **Shanghai A Share** and **Shanghai B Share**.)

Dow Jones Shenzen
An index of the **Shenzen Securities Exchange**. (See also **Shenzen A Share** and **Shenzen B Share**.)

Dow Theory
The New York Institute of Finance (NYIF) maintains that the Dow Theory, expounded by Charles H. Dow, underpins modern **technical analysis**. According to the NYIF publication, *Technical Analysis – A Personal Seminar* (Simon & Schuster, 1989) six of the Dow Theory's most basic tenets are:

a. The averages discount everything except acts of God;

b. There are three types of trends – major (long-term, more than a year), intermediate (mid-term, several weeks to several months) and minor (short-term, a week to several weeks);

c. The major trends go through three phases – accumulation, bull market and distribution;

d. The averages must confirm each other;

e. Volume must confirm the trend; and

f. Trends will continue until there is a definite signal of a reversal (in other words, what happens will continue to happen until it stops.)

DPS
dividend per share.

DRIP
di**vidend reinvestment plan**.

dual listing
a company that is listed on two **bourse**s.

duopoly
A situation where only two suppliers provide a product within an economy. An example might be a nation with two competing telephone companies. (See **monopoly**.)

E

E
The single letter code for Transco Energy, a company listed on the NYSE. (See **stock symbol**.)

earnings
net profit.

earnings margin
net profit of a company as a percentage of **turnover**.

earnings per share
The most often used yardstick of the earnings support underpinning a share. Just as many years ago, a single currency unit was expressed by the value of gold that underpinned it, the basic earnings per share represents the net earnings of a company that underpins each share.

$$EPS = \frac{\text{Net earnings (profit after tax and minority interest but before extraordinary items)}}{\text{Weighted average number of common shares outstanding}}$$

When attempting to compare the EPS figures of different companies it is fairer to use a **fully diluted EPS**.

Earwitness
A market intelligence column in **Malaysian Business** magazine, regarded as a must-read by Malaysian **stock market** punters.

ECU
European Currency Unit.

Edgewise
A market intelligence column in the Malaysian business weekly, *The Edge*, that enjoys a formidable following.

Edwards, Robert D.
Co-author with John **Magee** of the basic textbook of **technical analysis**, *Technical Analysis of Stock Trends* (John Magee Inc., 1992). The book is deemed the definitive work on pattern recognition analysis as applied to the **stock market**. Edwards and Magee's work expanded upon Charles **Dow**'s **Dow Theory**. Edwards developed the science of analysing pattern formations and **support-resistance** levels, and identifying trends.

effective tax rate
For an individual, it is his total personal tax charge for the year divided by overall income, shown in percentage terms.

For instance, if Mr. Loadsa De' Pendenz earns $90,000 a year and has allowances totalling $30,000, he only pays tax on $60,000. If that tax charge is worked out on a graduated scale he might pay 10% on his first $40,000 and 15% on the remaining $20,000. That would mean he gleefully forks out $4,000 + $3,000 = $7,000 in taxes. In working out his effective tax rate, take that $7,000, divide it by his total $90,000 income, and describe it in percentage terms. In this case, it comes to 7.8%, an extremely low effective tax rate.

For a corporation, it is its total tax charge divided by the year's pre-tax profit, again shown in percentage terms.

For instance, if Imaginative Accounting Pte Ltd has **accumulated tax credits** of $3m and a pre-tax profit for the year of $25m, only $22m will attract taxes at the prevailing corporate tax rate. Let us assume that tax rate is 25%. Imaginative Accounting then pays 25% of $22m or $5.5m in taxes. Its effective tax rate is worked out by taking its total tax charge of $5.5m and dividing it by the year's total profit of $25m, and expressing that in percentage terms. In this case that works out to 22%. (See **taxation**.)

Efficient Market Theory

Also known as the Efficient Market Hypothesis. It has three main forms, the **Weak Form, Semistrong Form** and the **Strong Form**. But in its broadest sense EMT simply suggests that stock prices reflect available information and therefore there is no way for extraordinary profits, out of line with general market appreciation, to be made.

Although the advent of computer-aided programmed trading has helped identify perceived over- and under-valued situations, the EMT has still at least been partially debunked by the phenomenal successes of the **Buffett**s and **Lynch**es (and hopefully the Yous) of the world.

This anecdote from the Preface of Haim Levy's textbook, *Introduction to Investments* (South-Western College Publishing, 1996), helps illustrate the perversity of EMT (particularly of the **Strong Form)** if taken to extremes:

> A university professor who wrote his doctoral dissertation on the topic of 'market efficiency' was walking past the New York Stock Exchange at 11 Wall Street with his ten-year-old son when suddenly the boy exclaimed, "Dad, there's a $100 bill on the sidewalk!" "That's impossible," retorted the professor, "the market is efficient and, in an efficient market, $100 bills cannot be found on the sidewalk!"

EGM

Extraordinary General Meeting.

EI
Extraordinary item – a line item in a company's profit and loss account (**P&L**) below its **net profit** line item.

ELSOS
Employee loyalty share option scheme. It differs from an **ESOS**, as here employees have to remain employed for several more years to qualify for these shares to be sold to them at a **discount**.

EMS
European Monetary System that has birthed the **ECU**, or European Currency Unit. The EMS is setting the stage for a full blown **EMU**.

EMT
Efficient Market Theory.

EMU
European Monetary Union that aims to fuse all the nations in the European Community, EC, into one fully integrated economic unit with the establishment of a European super **central bank**. In the minds of those committed to the establishment of the EMU, all European currencies will eventually be abolished and replaced by the European Currency Unit. (See **EMS**.)

entry PE
PE level that a company is bought at. (See **exit PE**.)

EPF
Malaysia's Employees' Provident Fund. (Also see **CPF**.)

EPS
earnings per share.

equities
The generic term for the realm of investments in **common stock**. (See **equity**.)

equity
At its most basic level it refers to an interest in ownership. Since ownership of even one **share** of the **common stock** of a company denotes proportional ownership, the **stock market** is often referred to as the equities market. (See **equity base**.)

equity base
The number of common stock shares making up the full ownership pie of a company. Both **bonus issue**s and **rights issue**s increase a company's equity base.

equity market
Another term for the **stock market**.

ESOS
employee share option scheme. (See **ELSOS**.)

ethics
Given the Biblical admonition that 'the love of **money** is the root of all evil', it is heartening to note that the **investment** community generally attempts to abide by a stratospheric level of self-governance. The fact that scoundrels and knaves abound does not detract from this sterling attempt but rather underscores its importance. A case in point is the **Code of Ethics** issued by the US-based Association for Investment Management and Research (AIMR) for **financial analyst**s which precedes a lengthy list of standards of professional conduct. Affiliated analysts around the world are expected to comply with the stringent AIMR guidelines.

European Monetary System
EMS.

ex
x. Without. (See **cum** and **ex-dividend**.)

ex-all
xa. Without everything. This denotes a **share** that no longer qualifies its purchaser to participate in whatever exercise or reward the company is planning in the near-term, such as **rights** or **dividend**s.

ex-bonus
xb. Same as **ex-capitalisation**.

ex-capitalisation
xc. Shares bought as xc shares do not qualify their purchaser to participate in an upcoming **bonus issue**.

exchange rate
The amount of one **currency** against one unit of another, most usually against the US **dollar**. (See **cross rates**.)

exchange-traded fund
A **closed-end fund** that is traded on an exchange.

ex-dividend
A stock that is trading without the right attached to it for a recently declared **dividend**. If two buyers of a stock, A and B, buy shares in a company, A before the ex-dividend date and B on the **ex-dividend date**, it is most likely that A paid more for his shares than did B. As soon as the ex-dividend date is reached, the market will rerate the shares downward to compensate for the loss in dividend income. In recompense for his higher purchase price, A qualifies for the dividend to be paid soon after, while B does not. (See also example under **cum**.)

ex-dividend date
If a buyer of a stock purchases it *on this date* or after it, he does not qualify to receive the recently declared dividend. (See **dividend** and **ex-dividend**.)

exercise
Choosing to do what is allowed by the terms of a financial instrument. In stock options trading, for instance, it would be the action taken by an owner to either buy or sell the underlying stock at the specified terms. If the owner or holder has a **call option**, exercising this would entail buying the underlying stock at the price specified by the call option. If he has a **put option**, exercising this would entail selling the underlying stock at the price specified by the put option. (See **writer**.)

exercise price
The price at which an **option** holder can, if he so chooses depending on market conditions and his own financial health, buy (or sell) the underlying stock in exercising a **call** (or **put**) **option**. The term 'exercise price' is interchangeable with **strike price**.

exit PE
PE level that a company is sold at. (See **entry PE**.)

expansion
Enlargement of a company's business scope through additional **capital expenditure**.

expiration date
In the financial world this is far more stringently applied than it is in your kitchen. While a loaf of bread or carton of milk can probably still be consumed a little after its expiration date, in options trading, for instance, the expiration date is the absolutely last day an option may be exercised.

ex-rights
xr. Shares bought as xr shares do not qualify their purchaser to participate in an upcoming **rights** issue.

extraordinary item
EI.

ex-warrants
xw. Shares bought as xw shares do not qualify their purchaser to participate in an upcoming **warrants** issue.

F

F
The single letter code for Ford, a company listed on the **NYSE**. (See **stock symbol**.)

face value
For **bond**s, the **nominal value** that represents the final payment at maturity, that is, on the **maturity date**.

Far Eastern Economic Review
Influential weekly regional business and political magazine. Commonly called '**FEER**' or simply 'the Review', established in Hong Kong in October 1946.

FDI
Foreign direct investment.

Federal Reserve System
The United States' monetary authority, and therefore the most powerful such entity in the world. It is commonly called **The Fed** in financial circles.

The Fed was set up in 1913. In keeping with Americans doing things in a bigger, if not always better, fashion the Fed is not one single **central bank** but rather a system of one dozen separate district banks. These are sprinkled across the continental US but tend to cluster on the eastern seaboard. The district banks are based in Atlanta, Boston, Chicago, Cleveland, Dallas, Kansas City, Minneapolis, New York, Philadelphia, Richmond, San Francisco and St Louis. The entire system is governed by its seven-member Board of Governors. The chairman, currently the powerful and much-respected Alan Greenspan, serves a four-year term.

FEER
Far Eastern Economic Review.

fiduciary
Someone who acts on behalf of another in financial matters, and has the obligation to do so with the best interests of that person in mind.

FIFO
The 'first in, first out' method of accounting for a company's inventory. (See **LIFO**.)

financial analyst
One who analyses **financial statements** for clues as to the state of health of a company. Although this term is sometimes used interchangeably with **investment analyst**, the financial analyst is usually deemed to have a more narrow focus and does not necessarily convey **investment** advice. (See also **Code of Ethics** and **analyst**.).

financial statements
Various company accounts like the **P&L** and **balance sheet** which when taken together help give a clear picture of a company's health, unless undetected **window dressing** has taken place.

Financial Times
Commonly called the **FT**. Britain's finest financial newspaper, clearly distinguished by its salmon pink paper. Some members of the

investment community look upon it as the definitive business paper of the world, for its breadth of coverage, balanced treatment that is looked upon as less pro-US than the **Wall Street Journal**'s, and the depth of analysis in its articles on global issues.

financial year
A company's **fiscal year**, which may or may not begin on January 1 and end on December 31. (When it does, the company's financial year is said to coincide with the calendar year.) But regardless of when it begins, the financial year is the basic time unit in which a company's annual performance is gauged. The primary **financial statements** of a company are prepared for each such period.

first in, first out
FIFO.

First Philippine Fund
Commonly denoted as **FPF**. This **closed-end fund** is listed on the **NYSE** and was launched in November 1989 by Clemente Capital. Its stated investment objectives are to ride on the long-term capital growth of the Philippines. Price and **NAV** data on **FPF** are readily found in the **AWSJ**. (See **mutual funds**.)

fiscal policy
budgetary policy.

fiscal year
The 12-month period for which a company's primary budget and earnings forecasts are assessed. (See **financial year**.)

Fisher, Philip A.
A pioneer of modern investment theory. Fisher began his career as a securities analyst in 1928. In 1958 his foundational book, *Common Stocks and Uncommon Profits*, was first published. Warren **Buffett** is counted among Fisher's many adherents.

Fisher's 15 Points
A remarkably concise set of 15 questions **Philip A. Fisher** posed in his most famous book, *Common Stocks and Uncommon Profits* (John Wiley & Sons, Inc., 1996), to help investors decide what stock to buy. (See **Fisher's Point 1** to **Fisher's Point 15**.)

Fisher's Point 1
Does the company have products or services with sufficient market potential to make possible a sizeable increase in sales for at least several years?

Fisher's Point 2
Does the management have a determination to continue to develop products or processes that will still further increase total sales potentials when the growth potentials of currently attractive product lines have largely been exploited?

Fisher's Point 3
How effective are a company's research and development efforts in relation to its size?

Fisher's Point 4
Does the company have an above average sales organisation?

Fisher's Point 5
Does the company have a worthwhile profit margin?

Fisher's Point 6
What is the company doing to maintain or improve profit margins?

Fisher's Point 7
Does the company have outstanding labour and personnel relations?

Fisher's Point 8
Does the company have outstanding executive relations?

Fisher's Point 9
Does the company have depth to its management?

Fisher's Point 10
How good are the company's cost analysis and accounting controls?

Fisher's Point 11
Are there other aspects of the business, somewhat peculiar to the industry involved, which will give the investor important clues as to how outstanding the company may be in relation to its competition?

Fisher's Point 12
Does the company have a short-range or long-range outlook in regard to profits?

Fisher's Point 13
In the foreseeable future will the growth of the company require sufficient financing so that the larger number of shares then outstanding will largely cancel the existing shareholders' benefit from this anticipated growth? (Examine the example in the **rights issue** entry.)

Fisher's Point 14
Does the management talk freely to investors about its affairs when things are going well but 'clam up' when troubles and disappointments occur?

Fisher's Point 15
Does the company have a management of unquestionable integrity?

Five Laws of Gold
George Samuel **Clason**'s character **Arkad** in the financial classic *The Richest Man in Babylon* (Penguin, 1988) gave these five laws to his son to teach him the way to wealth. (See **Clason's Law 1** to **Clason's Law 5**).

flat market
A **market** in which prices of the goods traded within it remain unchanged for a lengthy period.

Footsie
The appealing nickname of the Financial Times-Stock Exchange Index (**FT-SE Index**). It records price changes in 100 leading UK listed companies.

forced-sale
In the case of a **margin** purchase of an asset that then heads sufficiently south in price, this takes place if the client is unable or unwilling to provide a top-up of funds (the latter might take place if a **speculator** chooses to heed Fred **Tam**'s rule 'h' (of successful futures trading).

foreign exchange
Money held in the form of **currencies** other than that of the holder's country of origin. (See **exchange rate** and **cross rates**.)

forex
foreign exchange.

FPF
First Philippine Fund.

free-floating exchange rate regime
One of three main **exchange rate** categories. Under this regime the exchange rates of the currency in question are left completely to **market forces** with absolutely no government intervention. (See also **pegged exchange rate regime**, **managed floating exchange rate regime** and **currencies**.)

FT
The **Financial Times**.

FT-SE Index
Footsie, sometimes also called the FT-SE 100 Index.

fully diluted EPS
An **earnings per share** figure that is more representative than just the basic **EPS**, that assumes all **common stock** equivalents like warrants and options are fully converted, if they are exercisable in the year in question. When comparing different companies within a sector, it is best to do so on a fully diluted (or as is commonly shown in **investment** reports, FD EPS) basis since it reveals off **balance sheet** funding. Most of the time a fully diluted EPS figure is lower than a basic EPS, unless **interest** savings arising from conversion of the common stock equivalents filter back into a company's **earnings** (this is best modelled within the company's **cash flow statement** and exhibits itself in reduced interest charges) and more than compensate for the rise in the number of shares.

$$\text{F.D. EPS} = \frac{\text{Net earnings (profit after tax and minority interest but before extraordinary items) including interest savings from the conversion of the common stock equivalents}}{\text{Highest number of possible common shares outstanding in any year}}$$

fully invested
Given the truth of both the **Rainbow Effect** and the **Rip van Winkle Effect**, namely the immense difficulty in exactly figuring out which **stock** is going to move first or even when exactly an **investment** will pay off, it is generally agreed among **stock market** pundits that being fully invested in the stock market at all times is the surest way to enjoy the long-term benefits of large **compounding** effects.

fully valued
One way a **financial analyst** conveys his opinion that a particular **investment** is not likely to head **north** for a long time to come. It can be a euphemism for a **sell** recommendation.

fundamental analyst

As opposed to the **chartist**, this generally more respected member of the **investment** community utilises **fundamentals** in his perpetual search for that perfect **stock** – one trading well below its **book value per** share, with an **EPS** growth rate in the triple figures that is sustainable from here to eternity, and comes with a story compelling enough to whet the appetites of **institutional investor**s yet simple enough to be understood by his broking firm's **dealer**s.

fundamental analysis

The act of drilling down to the basics of a company and an industry in an attempt to determine if there is value in a particular **investment**. This stands diametrically opposite of **technical analysis**. (See also **Modern Portfolio Theory**.) Modern fundamental analysis has its roots in the work of Benjamin **Graham** (see **Security Analysis**) and found its most able and richest practitioner in the person of Warren **Buffett**.

fundamentals

Attributes of a company like its actual **earnings**, earnings potential, **asset** base and quality of management that if analysed carefully may result in smart **investment** moves.

fund manager

A money manager who runs a **mutual fund** or **unit trust**. Peter S. **Lynch** and Anthony R. **Gray** are just two such examples who have become famous by racking up enormous gains for their funds and then later writing about these exploits.

futures

General term for all futures traded contracts in commodities, stock derivatives or **indices**.

future value

The value at a specified point in the future of a set of cash flows stretching out from the present to that future point. If the future value (FV) is to be calculated using a set interest rate (I) acting on an initial cash flow now (Cfn) for a set period (P), the formula is:

$$FV = Cfn \times (1 + I)^P$$

So if you want to work out the future value of a $1000 investment today in 8 years' time if you earn 9% compound interest, plug the variables into the formula. FV = to be worked out; Cfn = $1000; I = 9% or 0.09; and P = 8 years.

$$FV = \$1000 \times (1 + 0.09)^8 = \$1000 \times (1.99256) = \$1,992.56$$

As can be seen in this example, the amount of money almost doubles in the period. A quick way of finding out how long a particular rate of compound interest needs to double your money is found using the famous **Rule of 72**.

Future value also comes into play in the more complicated case of working out how much an **annuity** will be worth at a specified point in the future.

If an annuity promises to pay at fixed periodic intervals, starting one unit of time out (be it one day, one month, one year, etc.), it is possible to work out its future value.

If the annuity promises to pay over the next P years, let's assume 8, starting next year, with set payments (PMT) each year of $90, then depending on the interest rate, I, it is possible to work out the future value of this annuity (FVA).

$$FVA = PMT \times [\{(1 + I)^P - 1\}/I]$$

In our specific example, we will assume I = 9%. This then works out to:

$$\begin{aligned} FVA &= \$90 \times [\{(1 + 0.09)^8 - 1\}/0.09] \\ &= \$90 \times [\{(1.99256) - 1\}/0.09] \\ &= \$992.56 \end{aligned}$$

(See also **investing**, **IRR**, **NPV** and **present value**.)

G

G
The single letter code for Gillette, a company listed on the **NYSE**. (See **stock symbol**.)

GAAP
Generally Accepted Accounting Principles.

gambling
Creating a risk where there was none before in the hope of beating the odds. Usually a mug's game.

Gardner, David and Tom
The two brothers who have created the most popular on-line investment club on the **Internet** called **The Motley Fool**.

Gaussian distribution
The **normal distribution curve** or **bell curve**. It derives its name from Karl Friedrich Gauss, a German, who lived from 1777 to 1855. Although he probably never met a **PE** ratio or dealt with **EPS** growth figures, he would undoubtedly have understood them if he had. In fact, the curve that bears his name in statistics is used constantly in **investment** circles as an aid to distribution analysis. Gauss made

such significant inroads in astronomy, physics and mathematics that there is a small, walled plain on the Moon named after him. (See **standard deviation**.)

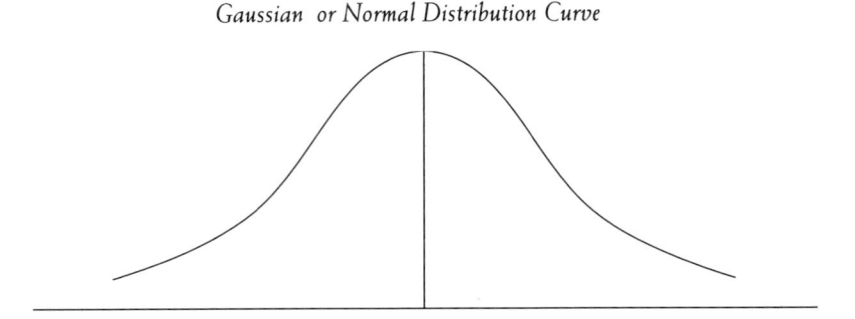

Gaussian or Normal Distribution Curve

GDP
Gross Domestic Product. This represents the aggregate output of a nation that is produced domestically. (See **GNP**.)

gearing
A company's debt to equity ratio. If gearing exceeds 1.0, the company in question appears to be excessively in debt. Generally speaking, the lower a company's gearing the more latitude it has to take advantage of fresh business opportunities.

A commonplace analogy would be the amount of slack you have on your credit card. If you are up to your eyeballs in hock with instalment debt, mortgage debt and consumer debt, you're not likely to be able to do very much about attractive **investment** opportunities that come your way.

general offer
GO (pronounced jee-o).

gilt-edged securities
High grade **bonds** or **preferred stock** issued by **blue chip** companies.

give (the buyer)
Sell now – at whatever lower price the buyer is offering. This is in direct contrast to **book (the seller)**.

GNP
Gross National Product. This represents the aggregate output produced by the domestic residents of a nation, regardless of whether they do so within that nation's borders or outside them. (See **GDP**.)

The relationship between **GDP** and GNP is best seen through the formula:

$$GNP = GDP + NIFA$$

where NIFA stands for net income from abroad. If a nation is a net provider of services abroad, then its NIFA is positive and its GNP exceeds its GDP. If a nation is a net importer of services from abroad, NIFA is negative and GDP then exceeds GNP.

GO
General offer. This occurs when a major shareholder breaches set limits in its stake of a listed company. For instance, in Malaysia the GO trigger level is 33.3% and in Singapore it is 25%. Once that level has been triggered the major shareholder must make an offer to the general public holding the other shares (hence the term, general offer) to buy those outstanding shares at a price determined by the appropriate **regulators**.

going long
Buying an **investment**.

going short
Selling an **investment** not already owned with the intention of buying it back later to square off the books.

gold
The precious metal most closely associated with riches. (See the **Five Laws of Gold**.)

gold bug
A hardcore investor who is in love with the metal.

government bonds
Long-term IOUs or **bond**s issued by a government to help finance a budget deficit. (See **Treasury bond**.)

Graham, Benjamin
Investment guru who discipled Warren **Buffett**. The co-author of *Security Analysis* (McGraw-Hill, 1989) with David Dodd. Graham also wrote another investment classic, *The Intelligent Investor* (Harpers & Row, 1986), and is deemed the father of modern **fundamental analysis**.

Gray, Anthony R.
A combination value investor cum growth stock picker who in 1991 finally beat Peter **Lynch**'s record of return in a decade-long investment period. Gray was born in Omaha, Nebraska, home of the world's greatest investor, Warren **Buffett**. In his book, *A Thousand Miles From Wall Street, Tony Gray's Commonsense Guide to Picking Stocks* (Macmillan, 1995), which he co-authored with Kurt Greenbaum, he clearly elucidates one version of a viable investment strategy for the 1990s. (But a close examination of **Gray's Deadly Sin 1** to **Gray's Deadly Sin 7** suggests that successful investing is more an artistic craft than a hard science.)

Gray's Deadly Sin 1
Don't be Dumb. (It is almost impossible to know if you are or not until after the event; hindsight is always 20–20.)

Gray's Deadly Sin 2
Don't be Ignorant. (Do your homework and gather sufficient information. Wisdom lies in knowing how much that is. Study the strategies of **Graham, Buffett, Lynch, Fisher, Gray** and other savvy investors and be humble enough to learn.)

Gray's Deadly Sin 3
Don't be Timid. (Again, do your homework, and then go with the strength of your convictions.)

Gray's Deadly Sin 4
Don't be Overconfident. (Linked to **Gray's Deadly Sin 2**, this occurs when you don't know enough but think you do – a little knowledge is a dangerous thing.)

Gray's Deadly Sin 5
Don't be Stubborn. (In one sense this is a trader's mentality of being willing to go with the flow and not hang on to a stock through hell and high weather, regardless. Long-term investors gain respect when their stubbornness pays off and notoriety when it does not. It's your call.)

Gray's Deadly Sin 6
Don't be Impatient. (Check your personality type and see if you have what it takes to be a long-term investor. Although **Gray**'s book suggests that he is more of a trader than **Buffett** or **Graham**, this piece of advice falls squarely within the long-term camp. See Graham and Dodd's comments under **Random Walk Theory**.)

Gray's Deadly Sin 7
Don't be Disillusioned. (Don't give up. Everybody makes mistakes in the market. The trick is to try and maintain a slightly better than even success rate.)

Great Depression, The
A period of low economic activity throughout the world which began in the twilight months of the 1920s and carried on throughout most of the 1930s. The start date is precisely marked in the history books as coinciding with the **Crash of October 1929**.

Greater Fool Theory
The most mentally unsatisfying, most demeaning reason, to invest in a particular stock. The basic premise of this theory is that although the **investment** is a **dog** there is a bigger fool out there somewhere who is willing to take it off your hands for a higher price.

greenback
The US dollar. In the middle of the American Civil War, in 1862, President Abraham Lincoln's government first issued paper money. The notes were called greenbacks quite literally because the reverse side was printed with green ink. The name has stuck, and today the greenback is a slightly more informal name for this de facto global currency.

greenmail
'Blackmail' of the corporate variety. A typical greenmail exercise involves a greenmailer buying up a significant stake in a company. The controlling shareholders then pay the greenmailer a **premium** on his shares to go away and leave the company alone.

greenmailer
One who indulges in **greenmail**. (Also see **White Knight.**)

grey market
An unofficial **market** in equities that usually arises just prior to a company's listing. Because trading has not commenced on the **bourse** concerned, an indication of fair price is arrived at by informal communication between brokers, eager buyers and potential sellers

who may already have confirmation of share allocations. The grey market price is usually a rough guide as to the initial price performance of a **counter**.

gross dividend cover

The number of times a company's earnings for the year can 'cover' its total gross dividend payments for that year. For instance, in the case of Cash Bulge Ltd (see **dividend** and **dividend cover**), if the company chooses to give 10 cents per share (from an **EPS** of 40 cents) back to its shareholders on a gross basis, the gross dividend cover is $40/10 = 4$ times. Note that this differs from the net dividend cover in that it does not take into account the chunk taken away by **taxation**. Another way of describing this relationship is to look at the inverse of the gross dividend cover. This is called the **payout ratio**.

Gross Domestic Product

GDP.

gross margins

Gross profit of a company as a percentage of **turnover**.

Gross National Product

GNP. (See **GDP**.)

growth in earnings per share

Percentage growth of **EPS** on a **Year-on-Year** basis.

growth in sales

Percentage growth of **turnover** on a **Year-on-Year** basis.

H

H

The single letter code for Harcourt General, a company listed on the NYSE. (See **stock symbol**.)

Hang Seng Index

The **benchmark index** of the **Hong Kong Stock Exchange**. (See also **All Ordinaries** and **Dow Jones HK Small Cap**.)

hedge

In its most general sense, it literally means to hedge your bets. In futures trading, to hedge would allow the dealer to lock in a future profit through complicated hedging mechanisms. In the **forex** markets, **MNC**s often hedge their expected profits from foreign subsidiaries so as to not suffer the ignoble fate of reaping huge profits in foreign currencies only to have them evaporate through unfavourable forex movements. For example, if Lion City Roars Ltd of Singapore has a Malaysian subsidiary, Hang Tuah Sdn Bhd, that does a brisk business in selling wavy swords, it might face the following scenario.

Say Hang Tuah makes a net profit of RM10m in 1998. If the exchange rate between S$ and RM is stable throughout the repatriation of profit period, at S$1 = RM1.80, then in Singapore dollar terms Lion City would rake in S$5.56m and have a lot to roar about. But if the Singapore dollar surges throughout the year and instead averages S$1 = RM2.00, the holding company would only see S$5m in profits flow its way. Roaring of a different nature may ensue.

But an appropriate hedge would allow Lion City Roars to lock in on RM1.80 for at least part of its expected profits.

In the options world, a hedge would entail the buying or selling of offsetting positions in options to guard against adverse price movements in the **underlying investment**.

HKSE
Hong Kong Stock Exchange.

hold
To continue to hang on to a **stock**, **bond** or any other **asset**. When an **investment analyst** makes a hold recommendation he expects the **investment** to perform in line with its **benchmark index**.

holder
The owner of a financial instrument like a fixed deposit certificate, **stock** or **option**. (See **risk to holder** and **risk to writer**.)

holding company
parent company.

Hong Kong Stock Exchange
Asia's third largest bourse, after Tokyo and Osaka. The HKSE is set to become China's third stock exchange when the British Colony reverts to China in 1997. (See **Hang Seng**, **All Ordinaries** and **Dow Jones HK Small Cap**.)

I

I
The single letter code for First Interstate, a company listed on the **NYSE**. (See **stock symbol**.)

IBM
International Business Machines, invariably referred to by its initials. For a long time considered the bluest of the America's blue chip companies, hence its nickname, Big Blue. The name has stuck although the company itself has had several recent years of lousy results. (See **Dow Jones Industrial Average**.)

IF
Indonesia Fund.

IGF
India Growth Fund.

illiquid
A condition when an **investment** is not readily traded because of either low or no volume. (See **illiquid stocks**.)

illiquid stocks
Similar to **boutique** ones. Generally no or low volume counters. Good luck to you if you need to sell a lot in a hurry.

IMF
Washington DC-based International Monetary Fund. Sister organisation of the **World Bank**.

income stock
A **stock** bought primarily for its high **dividend yield** and not for any large capital appreciation potential.

index
A numerical barometer of a market, also often called a **stock index**. For instance, the **DJIA**, the **STII** and the **KLSE CI**, are each an index and collectively called **indices**. Because most **fund manager**s have their performance measured against some **benchmark index**, **investment analyst**s tend to make recommendations on **investment**s (like **buy**, **hold**, and **sell**) not so much in terms of expected absolute gains, but rather in terms of expected relative performance against an index.

index funds
Mutual funds that comprise the stocks making up an **index** so that the funds' performance matches that of an appropriate index. Although it appears a rather mindless way of investing, the truth is that most **fund manager**s fail to match the performance of their **benchmark index**. Because of this, an index fund has the distinct advantage of at least 'doing better than average'.

India Growth Fund
Commonly denoted as **IGF**. This **closed-end fund** is listed on the **NYSE** and was launched in August 1988 by the Unit Trust of India. Its stated investment objectives are to ride on the long-term capital

growth of Indian listed companies. Price and **NAV** data on **IGF** are readily found in the **AWSJ**. (See **mutual funds**.)

indices
The plural for **index**.

Indonesia Fund
Commonly denoted as **IF**. This **closed-end fund** is listed on the **NYSE** and was launched in March 1990 by BEA Associates. Its stated investment objectives are to ride on the long-term capital growth of Indonesian listed companies. However, it does venture into other countries like Malaysia, the Philippines, Singapore and Thailand. Price and **NAV** data on **IF** are readily found in the **AWSJ**. (See **mutual funds**.)

inflation
The tendency for prices to continually balloon, therefore eroding the true purchasing power of **currency**. In the case of economic indicators like **GDP**, nominal GDP is usually more than **real GDP** because of the effects of inflation.

initial public offering
IPO.

inside information
Privileged information known only to **corporate insiders**. If this information is used by them to gain a trading or investment edge over the general public, it then becomes **insider trading/dealing**.

insider
A **corporate insider**.

insider trading/dealing
A situation when **corporate insider**s, such as the directors of listed companies, take advantage of information that the general public is

not yet privy to and deal on that basis. By buying or selling before the general pack gets wind of price sensitive information, a killing can be made.

While generally illegal, it is inordinately difficult to prove. In Malaysia, for instance, only one person (up to the time of this writing) has ever been indicted for this offence. (See **inside information** and **price sensitive information**.)

institutional investor
An **investor** with a lot of money, and therefore clout, as he invests for large institutions like **mutual fund**s, pension funds and **unit trust**s.

interest
The 'rent' paid for the use of money. Interest is paid by a borrower to a lender for the use of that money. (See **interest rates** and **usury**.)

interest rate risk
A type of **risk** that **bond** investors are particularly susceptible to because bond prices move in opposite directions to **interest rates** due to **yield** adjustments.

interest rates
Various rental rates for money determined by **demand and supply** for **currency**. (See **interest**.)

internal rate of return
Commonly called the **IRR**. In general, when assessing the viability of an **investment**, it is possible to determine the IRR by calculating the interest rate that will give an **NPV** of 0. The higher the IRR, the more attractive the investment is.

Now, let's take a look at the **annuity** example given in the **net present value** entry, where the annuity pays over 8 years, at yearly intervals starting next year, set payments of $90 a year. In the NPV example we used a 9% discount rate and assumed the annuity cost $400, to give an NPV of $98.13.

In this example, it is easy to work out the IRR by juggling the discount rate so that the NPV = 0. The judicious use of a spreadsheet package or even a decent calculator will show that the IRR in this case is approximately 15.2929%. When applied to a **bond**, the **IRR** is also called its **yield to maturity**. (See also **investing, future value, NPV** and **present value**.)

International Monetary Fund
IMF.

Internet
The globally-linked system of thousands of computer networks. It is literally a network of networks. The synergistic explosion of knowledge resulting from this inter-linking will certainly continue to transform the way the peoples of the world interact in the century to come. It is therefore ironic that this potentially powerful tool for peace and communication actually evolved from the interconnection of supercomputer sites across the United States during the Cold War when fears of Soviet nuclear attacks prompted a decentralisation of Uncle Sam's computerised system controlling its own set of nukes.

When universities jumped on the bandwagon, more peaceful uses for the various networks came into being. While not all services on the Internet, or Net as it is commonly referred to, are equally useful, there are enormous **investment** tracking systems that can be utilised by those in the know. Probably the most fun one is **The Motley Fool** site on America Online created by two wacky and savvy brothers, **David and Tom Gardner**. But on the Net, the excellent constantly rubs shoulders with both the slightly dodgy and the extremely suspect. So be aware that because policing the Net is a difficult task, acting on investment advice sourced from it can be fraught with more risk than usual. Recently in the **AWSJ**, Rob Bertram, a Pennsylvania regulator and chairman of the Offers and Sales on the Internet Committee of the North American Securities Administrators Association, said:

> The Internet has lowered the barriers to entry for everyone, including those who would perpetrate fraud on the marketplace.

("Danger Lurks for Investors Surfing Internet", Money & Investing section, September 13–14, 1996, *AWSJ*, p. 13)

(See also **WWW**.)

in-the-money

A pleasant situation where money can be made from exercising an **option** in accordance with its terms (see **in-the-money call option** and **in-the-money put option**). Because of this, the option itself, if traded, will be selling at a **premium** and its holder can choose to cash out of the option directly.

in-the-money call option

When the **strike** or **exercise price** is lower than the current market price of the underlying stock. Because the **call option** affords the **holder** the right to **buy** at a specified price, he can exercise his **option**, buy cheaply and sell immediately, should he so choose, to rake in a profit.

in-the-money put option

When the **strike** or **exercise price** is higher than the current market price of the underlying stock. Because the **put option** affords the holder the right to sell at a specified price, he can exercise that **option** and sell for more money than owners of the underlying stock can.

intrinsic value

In general, the basic, inherent value of an **asset**. This is usually impossible to define since value is linked with the interplay of **supply** and demand. However in the **options** and **equities** game, intrinsic value can be pinned down as the cash value in the difference between an option's exercise or strike price and that of the underlying stock.

inventory

A company's stock of saleable goods.

investing

The reallocation of **cash flows** over time with the aim of enjoying **capital appreciation** and increased future income flows. (See **future value**, **IRR**, **NPV**, **present value** and **investment**.) Because of his willingness to forgo the 'good things in life' now so as to have money to invest, an investor is making an attempt to have even more of those good things later on. The essence of successful investing is captured in the following story:

How I Made My Fortune
(by an unknown millionaire)

It was really quite simple. I bought an apple for five cents, spent the evening polishing it, and sold it the next day for ten cents. With this I bought two apples, spent the evening polishing them, and sold them for twenty cents. And so it went until I had amassed a few thousand dollars. It was then that I bought shares in Apple Computer Corporation and made ten million dollars.

(as told by Tod Barnhart, *The Five Rituals of Wealth*, HarperBusiness, 1995, p. 132)

investment

The use of money to make more money through **investing** in **equities**, **real estate** or **collectibles**. The aim of all investment, once you strip away fanciful definitions is best explained by Warren **Buffett** in response to a friend's letter asking for advice on mutual funds:

The objectives you mention in your letter mean nothing. That is all a lot of bull put out by the sponsors. Everyone has the same objective – to end up with more dough than they start with a minimum of risk.

(Roger Lowenstein, *Buffett – The Making of an American Capitalist*, Weidenfeld & Nicolson, 1996, p. 61)

(See also **Modern Portfolio Theory Assumption 5**.)

investment analyst

Although the term is sometimes used interchangeably with **financial analyst**, those in **investment** circles generally look upon an investment analyst as one who goes a step beyond the financial analyst by making actual recommendations. As such, an investment analyst can be described briefly as one who is constantly on the look out for money-making stocks (and other investment instruments) to investigate with the aim of making recommendations like **buy**, **sell** and **hold**. (See **Code of Ethics** and **analyst**.).

investment bank
merchant bank.

investor

A person who indulges in **investing**. Particularly one who does so in a reasonably rational way over a lengthy period of time. (See **speculator**.)

invisibles

Services, which by their very nature are invisible in stark contrast to visible items like palm oil, cars and cotton. Invisibles would encompass financial, banking and insurance services and tourism and transportation charges.

IOU
Stands for 'I Owe yoU', essentially what every **bond** is.

IPO
Initial Public Offering, the first time **share**s in a **company** are offered to the public through its initial listing on a **stock exchange.**

IPP
Independent power producer. (See **power purchase agreement**.)

IRR
internal rate of return.

issued share capital
paid up shares of a **company**.

J

J
The single letter code for Jackpot Enterprises, a company listed on the **NYSE**. (See **stock symbol**.)

Jakarta Growth Fund
Commonly denoted as **JGF**. This **closed-end fund** is listed on the **NYSE** and was launched in April 1990 by Nomura Capital Management. Its stated investment objectives are to ride on the long-term capital growth of listed Indonesian companies and also non-Indonesian companies that derive significant income from that country. Price and **NAV** data on **JGF** are readily found in the **AWSJ**. (See **mutual funds**.)

Jakarta Stock Exchange
The Indonesian bourse, **JSX**.

Jakarta Stock Exchange Composite Index
The **benchmark index** of the **JSX**.

JGF
Jakarta Growth Fund.

JSX
Jakarta Stock Exchange.

junk bond
A high-risk **bond** issued by a corporation that is not robustly established yet has at least the potential of becoming hugely successful. To compensate for the immense **risk** the bond owner accepts (of perhaps seeing the company go under leaving him with nothing more than fancy printed toilet paper) the typical junk **bond** carries with it a high **coupon rate**.

K

K
The single letter code for Kellogg, a company listed on the **NYSE**. (See **stock symbol**.)

Keogh plan
This is a tax-sheltered retirement plan in the US that is often mentioned in the context of financial and retirement planning. It is designed for self-employed Americans without pension plans.

KF
Korea Fund.

Kip
The currency of Laos. (See **currencies**.)

KLCE
Kuala Lumpur Commodity Exchange.

KLIBOR
Kuala Lumpur Inter-Bank Offered Rate.

KLOFFE
Kuala Lumpur Options and Financial Futures Exchange.

KLSE
Kuala Lumpur Stock Exchange.

KLSE CI
Kuala Lumpur Stock Exchange Composite Index. The **benchmark index** of the **KLSE**.

Korea Fund
Commonly denoted as **KF**. This **closed-end fund** is listed on the **NYSE** and was launched in August 1984 by Scudder, Stevens & Clark. Its stated investment objectives are to ride on the long-term capital growth of South Korean companies. Price and **NAV** data on **KF** are readily found in the **AWSJ**. (See **mutual funds**.)

KSE-100
The **benchmark index** of the Karachi Stock Exchange.

Kuala Lumpur Stock Exchange
Asia's fourth largest **bourse**, after Tokyo, Osaka and Hong Kong. The **KLSE** is actively traded by both Malaysians, and foreigners, especially Singaporeans many of whom find the more freewheeling investment environment of the KLSE a welcome relief from the tight controls of the **SES**. KLSE interest is also spurred by a preponderance of colourful corporate characters.

Kyat
The currency of Myanmar (Burma). (See **currencies**.)

last in, last out
LIFO.

launder
The process of cleaning 'dirty' crime-derived money by running it through the inter-linked financial markets and banking systems of the world, including offshore centres.

Leeson, Nick
One-time British boy wonder turned rogue trader who brought down the House of Barings in early 1995 through a series of ill-placed bets on the direction of the Nikkei-225 futures contract. Leeson carried out his escapades while based in Singapore. His downfall and that of Barings stemmed from a combination of lax controls on the British merchant bank's part, Leeson's wrong bets on the **index** through the adverse intervention of the Kobe earthquake and its damaging effects on the **Nikkei-225** index, and his attempts to continually cover up his losses while he bet more and more of Barings **asset**s in a vain attempt to make good. This caused the losses to mount dangerously until it finally wiped out Barings.

Leeson has become a favourite target in financial circles in the mid and late '90s with numerous writers taking pot-shots at him. One example found in Fred KH Tam's *Understanding KLCI Stock Index Futures*, attributes Leeson's fall to non-adherence to some of Tam's 10 golden trading rules. (See **Tam, Fred KH**.)

Lembaga Tabung Angkatan Tentera
LTAT.

Lembaga Urusan Tabung Haji
LUTH.

lemming
Member of a **mob** without a mind of his own when it comes to making rational **investment** decisions. The term is derived from the sad rodents of Northern Europe which make migratory pilgrimages which result in them plunging into the ocean to drown en masse.

leverage
The potentially hazardous use of debt to increase purchasing power. (See **margin** and **margin account**.)

liability
Anything owed by you that requires repayment. It stands in diametric opposition to an **asset**.

LIBOR
London Inter-Bank Offered Rate.

LIFFE
London International Financial Futures and Options Exchange.

LIFO
The 'last in, first out' method of accounting for a company's inventory. (See **FIFO**.)

line-up
Series of parked orders to either buy or sell a **counter**.

liquid assets
Assets that are either in cash or in kind that can readily be converted to cash, like **common shares**.

liquidation
Hardly ever has anything to do with water and flooding except in the case of painful jokes, see **Noah**. In business it is the process of selling off or liquidating the assets of a firm that has gone under and ceases to be a viable ongoing business entity. (Also known as **winding up**.)

liquidity
The level of available cash or of assets that can be turned into cash.

liquidity crunch
A precipitous drop in the amount of liquidity in any system, be it the banking system or the **stock market**.

listed company
A company that has its **common stock** traded on a **stock exchange**.

Livermore, Jesse Lauriston
The world's most famous **speculator** reputed to have been broke 20 times in his life, bouncing back all of 19 times. Livermore died impoverished. His exploits were recorded by Edwin Lefevre in his investment classic, **Reminiscences of a Stock Operator**, where the protagonist is named Larry Livingstone, a pseudonym for Livermore.

long
Buying an **asset**. In options it refers to a market position set up by the purchase of one **option** without a balancing sale being made at that point.

long position
Generally speaking, just going **long**.

long position (in an option)
Buying an **option** without a corresponding sale.

lost opportunity
A form of investment **risk**.

lot
See **board lot**.

LTAT
A major Malaysian **institutional investor**, the Armed Forces Superannuation Fund. In Malay it stands for **L**embaga **T**abung **A**ngkatan **T**entera.

LUTH
Another major Malaysian **institutional investor**, the Muslim Pilgrims' Fund. In Malay it stands for **L**embaga **U**rusan **T**abung **H**aji.

Lynch, Peter S.
One-time star fund manager of the Fidelity Magellan Fund. He retired and turned to writing. Three of his highly readable books (all co-written with John Rothchild, a *Time* magazine columnist) are: *One Up On Wall Street* (Penguin, 1989), *Beating the Street* (Simon & Schuster, 1994) and *Learn to Earn* (Simon & Schuster, 1995).

Lynch's formidable long-term track record for a return on a 10-year investment was beaten in 1991 by **Anthony Gray** of Florida's Sunbank Corporate Equity Fund.

Lynch's Rule

A yardstick espoused by Peter **Lynch** (although used long before him) in assessing the viability of a **stock** investment. Regardless of how high a company's **PE** is, Lynch considered it a good **buy** if projected **earnings** are anticipated to grow at a percentage rate higher than the PE multiple.

For instance, if company Slow Growth Ltd has a prospective PE of just 12 times but is only expecting an average **EPS** growth of 10% a year over the next three years, Slow Growth would not meet Lynch's Rule. However if Frantic Expansion Ltd has a sky-high PE of 50 times but can be safely assumed to boast an average EPS growth of 60%, Frantic Expansion's earnings will quickly catch up with its current price level and huge capital gains can be expected from it.

M

M&A
Standard term in corporate finance for mergers and acquisitions.

Magee, John
Co-author with Robert D. **Edwards** of the basic textbook of **technical analysis**, *Technical Analysis of Stock Trends* (John Magee Inc, 1992). The book is deemed the definitive work on pattern recognition analysis as applied to the **stock market**. Magee and **Edwards'** work expanded upon Charles **Dow**'s **Dow Theory**. And Magee emphasised three main technical principles – **stock** prices move in trends; the volume will move in tandem with a trend; and once established, a trend has its own inertia and will continue with force. The late Magee, an MIT graduate in engineering, resisted calls to forecast where the market would head, clearly realising that predicting **Mr Market**'s mood swings is a mug's game.

Makati Stock Exchange
The Philippines' junior exchange, which began operations in 1965. (See **Manila Stock Exchange**.) The Makati and Manila bourses were merged into the **Philippine Stock Exchange** in 1993.

Malaysia Fund
Commonly denoted as **MF**. This **closed-end fund** is listed on the **NYSE** and was launched in May 1987 by Arab-Malaysian Consultant Sdn Bhd. Its stated investment objectives are to ride on the long-term capital growth of Malaysian listed companies. Price and **NAV** data on **MF** are readily found in the **AWSJ**. (See **mutual funds**.)

Malaysian Business
A twice monthly magazine published in Malaysia that is considered a must-read by many investors and businessmen. Commonly referred to as MB, the magazine was established in October 1972. (See **Earwitness**.)

managed floating exchange rate regime
One of three main **exchange rate** categories. Under this regime the exchange rates of the currency in question see a degree of government intervention, although not to the extent seen in a pegged system. This regime falls half-way between the other two. Here, the government does not commit itself to maintaining any particular level of its currency against another major currency. **Bank Negara Malaysia** is active in the forex market because the **ringgit** operates in a managed floating exchange rate regime. (See also **pegged exchange rate regime** and **free-floating exchange rate regime** and **currencies**.)

managing director
In most companies the equivalent of the chief executive officer; the top gun, operationally speaking, in a **board**.

Manila Stock Exchange
The Philippines' senior exchange, established in 1927. It was the only stock exchange in the country until the establishment of the **Makati Stock Exchange**. Both were merged into the **Philippine Stock Exchange** in 1993.

margin

In equities, the portion of a stock's price that is actually paid for by a buyer, when his broking firm arranges to pay for the remainder on credit. This is more risky than buying completely with your own funds, and less risky than playing **contra**.

In futures, funds are required in a **margin account** to guarantee fulfilment of options contracts.

In both instances when an adverse price movement takes place, eroding the margin buffer, a top-up of funds is required. If a client is then unable or unwilling to provide the additional money, a **forced sale** usually ensues.

margin account

A client's account with a **brokerage** that contains the **margin** for **leveraged investment** purchases.

margin call

As a **margin** is essentially a leveraging device, when price movements occur that negatively affect the level of safety within a **margin account**, additional funds are required to top-up the margin of this now **undermargined account**. This addition is the margin call.

market

An arena of buyers and sellers. (See **market forces** and **markets**.) Most often used to refer to the **stock market**.

market capitalisation

In many ways this is the most important yardstick of a company's worth.

Current market capitalisation is rather easily worked out. Simply multiply the current share price by the number of **common shares** outstanding. The larger this number the more value the marketplace assigns to this **company**. So Company A with only 1m shares issued, with a current share price of $5, has a market capitalisation of $5m. Another, Company B with 10m shares issued, has a current share price of only 10 cents, and therefore a market capitalisation of $1m. The **market** has assigned A an economic value five times that of B.

This can be for various reasons: Company A may have better prospects, have huge untapped assets or be managed by well connected individuals, or B may be in a **sunset industry**, be bleeding or simply be an undiscovered gem waiting to be unearthed by some **investment** sleuth.

market forces
The dynamic set of interactions between buyers and sellers which rapidly decides upon the 'fair' price of goods and services. In the context of the **stock market** these are best viewed on a price screen with **bid**s and **offer**s constantly changing with the mood of investors, liquidity levels and news releases.

For instance, if Bloated Inc. is trading at $10 on projected future earnings of 50 cents a share (see **EPS**) then its **P/E** multiple is 20 times. If news leaks out that earnings will actually only come in at 25 cents a share because of increased competition in its main business areas, the stock will immediately begin to look expensive. As this realisation spreads like wildfire through the market, sellers will panic and buyers will be reluctant. A price drop driven by pure market forces will ensue. (See **demand and supply**.)

market order
An order to buy or sell a security at whatever the prevailing market price is. This means selling at the current **bid** or buying at the current **asked** price.

market player
Anyone involved in trading in any **market** whatsoever.

market rerating
When a country shows consistent signs of either a long-term improvement or decline in its economy, its **stock market** will undergo either an upward or downward rerating by the **investment** community. Generally, an upward market rerating means that investors are willing to pay more for stocks in the market. This will result in the average **PE** for the entire market rising. Conversely in the case of a downward market rerating the average PE drops because of selling pressure across the entire **bourse**.

markets
The various arenas that come about because somewhere, someplace, for every type of commodity or **investment** there are buyers looking for sellers, sellers looking for buyers and intermediaries who sometimes take a cut for bringing them together.

market timing
A facet of investing that is fraught with **risk**. Specifically an attempt by an **investor** or **speculator** to accurately predict the tops and bottoms of the **market** so as to absolutely maximise his gains. Part of the danger of market timing lies in the tendency to overtrade in a frenzy thus seeing hard won **capital gain**s evaporate in the form of mounting **commission** charges.

MAS
Monetary Authority of Singapore, the island republic's de facto **central bank**. Also the Malaysian national airline.

maturity date (of bond)
The date on which a **bond**'s **face value** or **nominal value** becomes payable by the issuer to the **holder** or owner.

May 13th
This date in 1969 when bloody race riots broke out in Malaysia. The **NEP** was put in place the following year as a means of economic and social reengineering to ensure the country never again falls into such grief.

MBO
Management Buy-Out. Usually done when the managers of a company decide to borrow a lot of money to purchase control of their company. This way they become owner-managers with a greater stake in the company's success than they had as mere employees.

MD
managing director.

memorandum of association
A document that declares to the public the name, registered address of a **company**, its share capital and details of the method of liquidation. It always goes in concert with the **articles of association**.

merchant bank
A bank that specialises in arranging funds as opposed to providing them. The value-added provided by a merchant bank comes from the expertise of its staff in investment management and corporate finance.

merger
A marriage of two corporate entities to create a larger, more formidable unit.

MF
Malaysia Fund.

MFCC
Malaysian Futures Clearing Corporation.

M-formation
The opposite of a **W-formation**. See **double top**.

MI
Minority interest. A line item in a **P&L account** sandwiched between **taxation** and **net profit**.

MME
Malaysian Monetary Exchange.

MNC
A standard abbreviation for any multinational corporation. This is any **conglomerate** that operates businesses in a host of countries and derives significant earnings from outside its home territory.

mob
In **investment** terms a mob refers to a crowd of **lemming**s.

Modern Portfolio Theory
MPT. Based on the **EMT**. This assumes the market is perfectly efficient and therefore it is impossible to consistently beat the market averages. Modern Portfolio Theory stands in direct conflict with the hopeful (and empirically proven) conviction underlying **fundamental analysis** that there are inefficiencies in the market and these can be utilised to find undervalued securities. There are 11 assumptions which underpin Modern Portfolio Theory. (See **Modern Portfolio Theory Assumption 1** to **Modern Portfolio Theory Assumption 11**.)

Modern Portfolio Theory Assumption 1
The **market** is efficient.

Modern Portfolio Theory Assumption 2
Investors hate **risk** and are only willing to take on more risk if greater **reward** is possible. (See **risk averse**.)

Modern Portfolio Theory Assumption 3
Investors would rather make more money than less.

Modern Portfolio Theory Assumption 4
Return and **risk** rise and fall in tandem.

Modern Portfolio Theory Assumption 5
Investors will try to make the most money with the least **risk**. (See **investment**.)

Modern Portfolio Theory Assumption 6
Investors always make their decisions based on two criteria: how much money can be made and how much **risk** must be assumed to make that amount.

Modern Portfolio Theory Assumption 7
It is possible to figure out just how closely linked any two investments are in their relative performance.

Modern Portfolio Theory Assumption 8
The more diversified an investor's **portfolio** is, the less **risk** is assumed but at the cost of making less money.

Modern Portfolio Theory Assumption 9
The investor's main reason in life is to figure what **asset** mix within his **portfolio** will give him a set **risk** level.

Modern Portfolio Theory Assumption 10
When trying to work out how much **risk** must be assumed to make a certain amount of money, an identical period of time is used in the calculations of each scenario.

Modern Portfolio Theory Assumption 11
All possible **investment**s are easily added to and subtracted from a **portfolio** in any **currency** amount.

M-o-M
See **Month-on-Month**. (Also see **Y-o-Y**.)

monetary tightening
Steps taken by a government through its **central bank** to reduce monetary **liquidity** by ratcheting up **interest rates** or by increasing the statutory reserve requirements (SRRs) of the country's banks so that they need to keep more money within the system without being able to lend it out.

money
A store of value and readily accepted medium of exchange which facilitates trade. (See **currencies**.)

money broker
A company that acts as a **broker** or middle man in transactions involving large sums of **money**, **forex**, **bond**s or any form of government paper, usually between banks or large corporations. Unlike a **discount house** that would make its money from the **spread** between the **discount** of the paper it deals in and its **face value**, a money broker only makes money on fixed **commission**s, much like a **stock broker** would. By the same token, a money broker would be out of a job in an environment of total **disintermediation**.

money manager
fund manager.

money market
A short-term investment arena. While the equities market tends to channel more 'long-term' funds for investment, for at least a few days, the **central bank** and the merchant and commercial banks of a country form the money market when they interact to determine short-term rates for periods as brief as overnight. Therefore, money market interest rates reflect the **demand and supply** for short-term funds and also factor in expectations of near-term interest rate movements.

money market funds
Mutual funds that invest in short-term financial securities. In countries where these are available they represent a potentially higher yielding alternative to conventional bank savings accounts. (See **passbook rate**.)

monopoly
Sole supplier of a product within an economy. (See **duopoly**.)

monopsony
Sole buyer of a product within an economy.

Month-on-Month
A comparison of economic or financial data that looks at the percentage change over the preceding one-month period. For instance, a **M-o-M** increase in car sales of 2% in May, 1997, means that one-fiftieth more cars were sold in May, 1997, than were sold in April, 1997. (See **Year-on-Year**.)

Month to date
Same as **Month-on-Month**. (See **Year to date**.)

moratorium
A set time period in which a specified activity cannot take place. For instance, major shareholders may be subject to a moratorium on the sale of their shares for three years after the **IPO** of their **company**.

moving average
A calculated mean figure that operates loosely along the same lines as the **FIFO** inventory method, in the sense that the first or oldest numbers in a series get thrown out first. For instance, a 30-day moving average of the closing price of a stock will take the average of the last 30 days. At the end of the next trading day, that day's new price level will be added to the series, and the oldest number of the series will be thrown out.

Another way of looking at it is analogous to viewing a linear series through a rectangular cardboard frame. As the window is moved from left to right the old numbers to the left are removed from sight and new numbers come in view. A constantly recalculated average of the numbers seen within the 'moving' frame is a moving average.

Moving averages are used in **stock** price analysis because they are an easy way of averaging the most recent price data, and are a favourite tool of the **chartist**.

MPT
Modern Portfolio Theory. (See also **Modern Portfolio Theory Assumption 1** to **Modern Portfolio Theory Assumption 11**.)

Mr Market
An allegory originally taught by Benjamin **Graham** to his students, including Warren **Buffett**. In Robert G. Hagstrom, Jr's *The Warren Buffett Way – Investment Strategies of the World's Greatest Investor* (John Wiley & Sons, 1994), he describes this 'person':

> To understand the irrationality of stock prices, imagine that you and Mr Market are partners in a private business. Each day without fail, Mr Market quotes a price at which he is willing either buy your interest or sell you his. The business that you both own is fortunate to have stable economic characteristics, but Mr Market's quotes are anything but. For you see, Mr Market is emotionally unstable. Some days Mr Market is cheerful and can only see brighter days ahead. On these days, he quotes a very high price for shares in your business. At other times, Mr Market is discouraged and, seeing nothing but trouble ahead, quotes a very low price for your shares in the business.
>
> Mr Market has another endearing characteristic, said Graham. He does not mind being snubbed. If Mr Market's quotes are ignored, he will be back again tomorrow with a

new quote. Graham warned his students that it is Mr Market's pocketbook, not his wisdom, that is useful. If Mr Market shows up in a foolish mood, you are free to ignore him or take advantage of him, but it will be disastrous if you fall under his influence. (pp. 50–51)

Not falling under the influence of Mr Market is probably the primary advantage of generally adopting a **buy and hold** investment strategy.

multinational corporation
MNC.

municipal bonds
IOUs or **bond**s issued by municipalities like towns and counties to help finance public construction projects like bridges and schools when the general operating budget is in deficit.

Munir Majid, Datuk Dr
Chairman of Malaysia's **SC**.

munis
See **municipal bonds**.

Murphy's Law
If anything can go wrong it will. Particularly in **investment**s if viewed in the short-term, especially if you are a **contra** player.

mutual fund
Similar to a **unit trust**, a mutual fund pools the 'mutual' resources of various investors and places them in an array of investments. A top-notch mutual fund manager, like the legendary Peter **Lynch**, once of mutual fund giant Fidelity Magellan has proven that it is possible to beat market averages, though that by no means suggests it is easy to do so. (See **Efficient Market Theory**.) There are two species of mutual funds – **open-end fund**s and **closed-end fund**s.

N

N
The single letter code for Inco Ltd, a company listed on the **NYSE**. (See **stock symbol**.)

NAFTA
North American Free Trade Area.

naked option
An **option** for which a **writer** holds no underlying stock to cover his obligation. This species of option is also naturally enough called an **uncovered option**.

naked writer
See **writer of a naked option**.

NASD
America's National Association of Securities Dealers.

NASDAQ
National Association of Securities Dealers Automated Quotations. It is a computerised exchange used by **dealer**s in the **OTC** market in the US.

National Association of Securities Dealers Automated Quotations
NASDAQ.

NAV
net asset value.

NBV
net book value.

NEP
New Economic Policy.

net asset value
Commonly abbreviated by analysts to **NAV**, this signifies the current value of all **asset**s of a **company** minus all its **liabilities**. (Similar to **net book value**.)

In the case of a **mutual fund** or **unit trust** the NAV represents the intrinsic value of a fund calculated simply by aggregating all market values of its underlying securities and netting off any outstanding fund liabilities.

net asset value per share
Net asset value / number of shares outstanding.

net book value
Same as **net asset value** unless a **company** intentionally holds certain appreciated **asset**s in its books under the original cost of acquisition. This might be the case in prudent property development companies.

net cash position
The final cash position ascertained in a **cash flow statement** after all actual cash inflows and outflows are calculated.

net change in cash

An intermediate number arrived at in a **cash flow statement** that quantifies the net change in the cash position for an entire fiscal year. For instance, if the **net cash position** for **fiscal** or financial year 1997 is $5.3m, and the net change for 1998 is a depletion of cash reserves by $2.3m, the net change is denoted as −$2.3m. The calculated net cash position for fiscal year 1998 is then $3.0m:

$$\text{net cash position} = [\$5.3m + (-\$2.3m)]$$

net current assets
current assets − current liabilities.

net debt
total liabilities − total assets.

net debt to equity
A ratio arrived at by dividing **net debt** by total shareholders' funds or **shareholders' equity**.

net dividend cover
The number of times the annual **dividend** declared by a **company** to the **shareholder** of one **share** (after taxes have been taken out) is 'covered' by the **EPS**. The calculation is simple: EPS/net **DPS**.

No particular net dividend cover ratio is inherently good or bad. Each company should be assessed in its own right. But in general, if the ratio is too low (1 or less than 1) the company would appear to be eschewing the active pursuit of growth for immediate reward of its shareholders. This may be justified in companies in a **sunset industry**.

If the net dividend cover is too high, it signifies that the **board** is reluctant to pay out too much of a company's earnings. The money might be retained to fund future growth of the company. A general rule of thumb is to determine if the management is able to create more than $1 of shareholders' wealth for every $1 retained. If it can, it is justified to pay out small or even no dividends. A classic case of such is Warren **Buffett**'s flagship **Berkshire Hathaway** that has not declared a dividend since 1967 (when it paid out US$0.10 a share). But since then its share price has just soared and soared and soared. For instance, Berkshire's shares began 1990 below US$9,000 and closed at US$38,000 on April 29, 1997. In this instance, it can safely be said that shareholders' wealth has been created and no one within Berkshire's register complains of the infinite net dividend cover (mathematically, any non-zero number divided by zero tends to infinity).

net present value

Is equal to the total **present value** of all future cash flows but with one addition, namely the (negative) cost of the **investment** or the initial cash outlay.

Looking at the example given in the **present value** entry, note that if the **annuity** promises to pay over the next 'm' years, 8 in that example, at yearly intervals starting next year, set payments (PMT) each year, of $90, and with the interest rate, I, assumed at 9%, it is possible to work out the present value of this annuity (PVA).

$$PVA = PMT \times [(1 - \{1/(1+I)^m\})/I]$$

In our specific example, this works out to:

$$PVA = 90 \times [(1 - \{1/(1+0.09)^8\})/0.09] = \$498.13$$

If the annuity actually costs $400 to buy today, then its NPV is

$$\$498.13 - \$400.00 = \$98.13.$$

The principle also holds true when the cash flows are not the same in each period. Then each one must be discounted separately and the summed. This can be done using the formula for present value, namely,

$$PV = Cfm/(1+I)^m$$

and applying it for various 'm' values running from 1 to the last period to be considered. The total present value then becomes the sum of all the different PV entries worked out using the basic formula.

Then because the NPV involves the initial cash outlay, an additional summation must be done for m = 0, where the amount forked out is a negative number.

Therefore,

$$NPV = \sum_{m=0}^{m=n} Cfm/(1+I)^m$$

With 'm' running from 0 to the last period (n) considered. (See also **investing, future value, IRR** and **present value**.)

net profit (earnings)
profit before tax − tax − **MI**.

net profit margin
[(net profit × 100) / turnover]%. If this rises from year to year, it would suggest that the company is doing many things right to reduce wastage and enhance its business viability. Of course, it all means nothing if the absolute net profit figures are not also rising.

net tangible assets
Shareholders' equity minus intangible assets (like goodwill).

net tangible asset backing per share
net tangible assets/number of shares outstanding.

net worth
Of an individual is the final figure one gets after assessing the market value of all his **assets** minus all his **liabilities** or debts.

New Economic Policy
A successful 20-year Malaysian programme of wealth redistribution that was put in place in 1970. It continues in another form today,

with the primary aim of redressing economic imbalances between the three main ethnic groups – the Malays, Chinese and Indians – that triggered the **May 13th** series of race riots in the first place.

neutral stock
A **stock** with a **beta** of 1.0.

New York Stock Exchange
The **NYSE** or **Big Board**.

Nikkei-225
The globally accepted **benchmark index** of the Tokyo Stock Exchange. (See **Topix Index**.)

Noah
The most **savvy** businessman of the ancient world. He floated his **stock** while the rest of the world underwent **liquidation**.

nominal value
For **common stock**, the nominal value of a share has no bearing at all on the intrinsic or even perceived worth of that share. For instance, in most countries the nominal value of a share is one unit of its currency, say RM1 or S$1. The current value of the share can (rarely) be at the nominal value, or (more likely) be anything above or below the nominal value. However, the nominal value, or **face** or **par value**, does have its use in that it helps to readily describe how a company's **paid up capital**, as opposed to **market capitalisation**, is represented.

For **bond**s, the nominal value represents the final payment at the **maturity date**. Also, the **coupon rate** is stated as a percentage of the nominal value.

normal distribution curve
A simple bell-shaped curve that remarkably describes many complex real life situations such as the distribution of heights in a population

of men aged 23 to 34, the amount of money in bank accounts around the country, the return on a universe of stocks or the IQs of the inmates of your local zoo.

A normal distribution curve is mathematically described as

$$f(x) = ce^{-(1/2)[(x-a)/b][(x-a)/b]}$$

and is clearly well beyond the purview of this book (thankfully, due to the mathematical limitations of this writer). Suffice it to say this function looks like a bell and is terribly useful. Also called the **bell curve** or **Gaussian distribution.** (See **standard deviation**.)

normal growth firm
A company that grows at a pace in line with the national economy.

north
Rising prices in a **market**. As in 'prices head north'.

no volume
No (substantial) business on an exchange!

NPV
net present value.

NTA
net tangible assets.

NYSE
New York Stock Exchange. The oldest, most established of America's three largest bourses. The other two are **AMEX** (nothing to do with the card) and **NASDAQ**. Companies listed on the NYSE are generally deemed to have 'arrived'.

It is probably the most important bourse in the world. In the aftermath of the **Crash of October 1987** there was introduced a braking mechanism if the market falls too much in a single session.

According to *The Wall Street Guide to Understanding Money & Investing*:

> If the **DJIA** falls 250 points, the NYSE closes for an hour. If the drop hits 400 points when trading resumes, it shuts down for two hours. The financial futures markets close down when stocks drop about 160 points.
>
> That means a crash would almost certainly be drawn out over several days. Since investor panic makes any crash worse, slowing down the pace of the fall should help deter hasty sell decisions. (p. 73)

NZSE-40 Index
The **benchmark index** of the New Zealand Stock Exchange.

O

October

The month many investors and speculators tend to get leery of the **stock market**. See **Crash of October 1929**, **Crash of October 1987**, and **Great Depression**. Mark Twain didn't help the reputation of this maligned month much – though he did show a well-developed egalitarian streak – when he touched on dicey periods to indulge in **speculation** in Chapter 13 of *Pudd'nhead Wilson*:

> October. This is one of the peculiarly dangerous months to speculate in stocks in. The others are July, January, September, April, November, May, March, June, December, August, and February.

odd lot

A certain number of shares below the **board lot** size. An odd lot stock transaction usually carries with it higher commission rates due to the inconvenience to the broker.

offer

The price at which someone is willing to sell an asset. (See **asked** and **offer for sale**.)

offer for sale
An official indication of the willingness of someone to sell an **asset**. (See **offer**.)

offer price
The **offer**.

Old Lady of Threadneedle Street
An affectionate nickname for the **Bank of England**.

open-end fund
A **mutual fund** that continually sells as many units of itself as investors want. The Fidelity Magellan Fund (once managed by mutual fund superstar Peter S. **Lynch**) is one such fund. In an open-end fund the number of units outstanding rises and falls depending on whether there is a net buying or selling of its units by a constantly shifting population of holders. A **unit trust** is an open-end mutual fund. Its price moves strictly in line with the **NAV** of its **portfolio** only, there is no price component attributed to **demand and supply** of the open-end fund's units. (See **closed-end fund**.)

open outcry
While most modern exchanges are fully computerised with **bid** and **ask** levels being entered directly into an electronic trading system, older exchanges tend to still utilise the exciting dynamics of tangible human intervention. In an open outcry system traders scream at each other and signal actively to complete trades.

open position
An open account for either a **contra** play or for **pick-up**.

opening price
The price at which the first trade of an investment in any one trading session is transacted.

opening purchase
In options trading, the initial buying transaction which gives the **holder** a **long position**.

opening sale
In options trading, the initial selling or writing transaction which gives the **holder** a **short position**.

opening transaction
The very first trade done during a single session of a **market**.

option
An instrument that allows its owner the right, though not the obligation, to either buy or sell its **underlying investment** at a set price within a stipulated time frame. Because of the set period that an option can be exercised in, it is a prime example of a **wasting asset**. (See **call option** and **put option**.)

ordinary shares
common shares or common **stock**.

OTC
Over-the-Counter. This is the general term for the entire arena in which generally **illiquid stocks** not listed on any regular exchange can be bought or sold. That is not to imply that the OTC does not form a **market**. It does, but an OTC market is distinct from a regular exchange which boasts a 'floor' or at least a central location which forms the heart of a conventional exchange like the **NYSE**, **KLSE** or **SES**. In contrast OTC markets like **NASDAQ**, **SESDAQ** and **CLOB** comprise purely telephone and computer linkages between licensed dealers who move stocks between buyers and sellers through their own brokerage's computer systems.

out-of-the-money

A sad situation in option trading where the underlying **stock** is worth more than the **option**. (See **out-of-the-money call option** and **out-of-the-money put option**).

out-of-the-money call option

When the **strike price** or **exercise price** is higher than the current market price of the underlying stock. Because the **call option** affords the **holder** the right to buy at a specified price, though not the obligation to do so, a rational holder will not choose to exercise his out-of-the-money call option as he can buy the underlying stock for less in the open market.

out-of-the-money put option

When the **strike price** or **exercise price** is lower than the current market price of the underlying stock. Because the **put option** affords the holder of the option, who in this case will also own the underlying stock, the right to sell the stock at a specified price, though not the obligation to do so, a rational holder will choose not to exercise his out-of-the-money put option as he can sell the underlying stock for more in the open market.

oversubscribed

A happy situation for the **board** of a **company**, the vendors of its **share**s and its **underwriter**s, when an **IPO** draws more interest than is needed. For instance, if 10m shares are on offer and applications account for 97m, the shares are oversubscribed. The **over-subscription rate** is 8.7 times, a figure that is often miscalculated in the press.

oversubscription rate
A ratio that precisely quantifies how many times an **IPO** is **oversubscribed**. It is worked out rather easily, [{(number of shares applied for)/(number of shares on offer)} − 1] times.

Over-the-Counter
OTC.

P

P

The single letter code for Phillips Petroleum, a company listed on the **NYSE**. (See **stock symbol**.)

paid up capital
Nominal value x **paid up shares**. (See **authorised capital**.)

paid up shares
Issued shares, as opposed to those that are authorised but not issued. (See **authorised shares**.)

Pakorn Malakul Na Ayudhya
The chief of the Thai **SEC**.

PAP
People's Action Party, Singapore's ruling political party.

paper loss
A hopefully temporary situation when the quoted price of an **investment** is below what was paid for it. In such a situation it may be wise to exercise patience or conversely to mull over **Tam**'s rules 'c' and 'd'.

paper profit
A happy situation when the quoted price of an **investment** is above what was paid for it. In such a situation consider **Tam**'s rules 'c' and 'i'.

par value
nominal value.

parent company
The **holding company** of a group of subsidiaries and associates. (See **subsidiary** and **associate**.)

pari passu
Latin for 'equal pace' or 'progress' and therefore 'side by side'. This has been extended to the realm of **equities** to refer to new **share**s that carry with them all the rights of old ones, including recently declared **dividend**s.

par value
Face or **nominal value**.

passbook rate
The relatively low **interest rate** paid by a typical bank's savings account. (See **money market funds**.)

passive investment strategy
Any investment strategy, like **buy and hold**, that does not advocate overtrading or constantly reacting to the mood swings of **Mr Market**.

Pataca
The currency of Macao. (See **currencies**.)

payout ratio
The inverse of a company's **gross dividend cover**. It is worked out by taking the gross dividend a company pays out in a year and dividing that by its **earnings**. In the case of Cash Bulge Ltd which

we met in the **dividend cover** and **gross dividend cover** entries, the payout ratio is = 25%. This is worked out by taking the gross dividend per share, of 10 cents, and dividing it by the EPS, which we assume is 40 cents. If a company's payout ratio is too high, it might be an indication that it is not retaining sufficient earnings to fund future growth. On the other hand, it may be just what is required by an **investor** willing to sacrifice future capital appreciation in a company's share price in exchange for a high **dividend** income.

PE, P/E, PER
price earnings ratio. The formula:

$$PE = \text{price of each share} / EPS$$

The PE is a simple positive number that represents the number of years of current earnings an **investor** is willing to pay for a **share**. It is therefore nonsensical to calculate a negative PE from a 'loss per share' figure. Another way of looking at the current PE ratio is to realise it is the number of 'dollars' **Mr Market** is now willing to pay for each 'dollar' of earnings.

PE ratios usually fall into two categories, historical and prospective. For **investment** purposes, the latest historical one has less bearing than the immediate prospective one. Generally speaking, if two companies in the same industry with identical earnings growth prospects are trading at different PE ratios, the one with the lower PE would appear to be cheaper. But by **Lynch's Rule**, if the expected percentage growth of EPS is higher than the PE multiple, then it is worth paying that PE for a company. For instance, if company Fast Track Ltd is currently trading on a historical PE of 96 times and on prospective PE ratios of 48 times and 24 times for the next two financial years, it would appear that its **EPS** for both those years is doubling and then doubling again. That works out to 100% EPS growth for each of the next two prospective years. By Lynch's rule because the 100% average EPS growth figure (100) is more than the historical PE ratio (96), Fast Track would appear a sound **buy**.

The PE is the most commonly used valuation tool of an **investment analyst**.

pegged exchange rate regime

One of three main **exchange rate** categories, also called a fixed exchange rate regime. Under such a regime the exchange rates of the currency in question are kept under tight controls (to stay close to a pegged level against some major foreign currency like the US dollar) by the government. Usually a government will instruct its **central bank** to undertake market intervention activities using the country's international reserves of foreign exchange.

This inflexible pegging can put an inordinate strain on a country's foreign exchange reserves. In 1982, Mexico went through a difficult time. Prior to that devaluation crisis the pegged system naturally precipitated an avalanche of currency substitution out of Mexican pesos to greenbacks. To quote from Francisco and Luis Rivera-Batiz (*International Finance and Open Economy Macroeconomics*, Macmillan, 1989):

> Currency substitution between Mexican pesos and dollars was to a large extent in the form of dollar deposits at banks located in Mexico, that is, Mexidollars. Being afraid that the banks would export their Mexidollars in the event of a scare regarding possible exchange controls, and given the importance of Mexidollars in financing transactions of firms and individuals trading with Mexico, the Mexican government decided to avoid taking any risks and went ahead and nationalised the banks during the crisis. This created, of course, other types of disruptions in the local financial markets*, but it serves well to illustrate the significance of currency substitution in economies under fixed exchange rates. (pp. 487–488)

> *Currency substitution in Mexico and its interconnections with the crisis of 1982 have been examined by G. Ortiz, "The Dollarization of Mexico: Causes and Consequences," in P. Aspe, M. Obstfeld, and R. Dornbush, eds., *Financial Policies and the World Capital Market:*

The Problem of Latin American Countries (Chicago, Illinois: University of Chicago Press, 1983).

(See also **free-floating exchange rate regime**, **managed floating exchange rate regime** and **currencies**.)

Permodalan Nasional Bhd
PNB.

Peso
The Philippine **currency**. (See **currencies**.)

Philippine Stock Exchange
The sole Philippine **bourse** formed in 1993 through a merger of the senior **Manila Stock Exchange** and the junior **Makati Stock Exchange**.

Philippine Stock Exchange Composite Index
The **benchmark index** of the **Philippine Stock Exchange**.

PI
portfolio insurance. (See **stock index futures contract**.)

pick-up
Going through with a stock transaction and buying it within the **contra** period.

P&L
Profit and Loss Account. One of the two most important financial statements of a company. The P&L tracks all of a company's dealings throughout the course of a period (usually for its entire financial year) and arrives at a final 'score' as to how it did – the profit or loss for the year. Usually a large profit indicates a win, and a loss that the company saw defeat in that year's battle against the vagaries of the general economy. (See **balance sheet**.)

PNB
Permodalan Nasional Bhd. This Malaysian company was incorporated as a wholly-owned **subsidiary** of a body known as Yayasan Pelaburan Bumiputra (The Bumiput(e)ra Investment Foundation) to be a vehicle to promote **bumiputra** ownership of Malaysia's corporate wealth. PNB is direct product of the **NEP**.

portfolio
A collection of **investment asset**s held by one **investor** for the purpose of **risk**-reduction through **diversification**.

portfolio insurance
PI. (See **stock index futures contract**.)

position
Any contract that has been bought or sold. In **option**s trading a position can be liquidated in one of four ways. Through a **closing purchase**, **closing sale**, exercising it (see **exercise**), or by letting it expire (see **expiration date**).

Pound Sterling
The currency of the United Kingdom. (See **currencies**.)

power purchase agreement
PPA. In the process of privatising a nation's electricity generation business, it is normal for **IPP**s to be set up. The economic viability of any IPP hinges upon the details of its power purchase agreement with the primary power utility. It is therefore vital for those investing in the power sector of a country to understand the details of the various PPAs in effect. For instance, in Malaysia, power behemoth, Tenaga Nasional Bhd, has power purchase agreements with many IPPs, like YTL Power, Segari Energy Ventures, Powertek, PD Power and Genting Sanyen among others, that spell out how much power the mega utility will buy from each of the new entrants and at what

price. For a power **analyst**, the details of each PPA will impact earnings of the main utility and its smaller suppliers.

PPA
power purchase agreement.

preference shares
Shares that have a claim on a company's **assets** before **common shares** in the case of a **liquidation**. Also **dividends** (generally low and fixed) are paid first on these shares before common share dividends are declared.

preferred stock
preference shares.

premium
The amount, either in monetary or percentage terms, that a **stock** or **bond** trades at above a set mark. That mark can be its initial issue price, the market average **P/E** or even an industry average **P/E**. (See **discount**.) It can also refer to the amount above its **par value** that a stock is offered for sale.

Also, in **options** trading, the option's price is called the premium.

present value
Because the heart of investing involves the reallocation of **cash flows** over time with the aim of enjoying **capital appreciation** and increased future income flows, it is theoretically possible to make a stab at figuring out the present value of an **investment**. In essence it means determining, in the light of your assumptions, 'what that investment is worth today'. Once a conservative assessment of present value (PV) is determined, a rational investor will then be willing to pay less than the PV in the aim of making a profit or **capital gain**.

present value

Unlike the **future value** of an investment which gives the value in the future of a set of cash flows stretching from the present to the future, present value takes the same set of future cash flows and discounts them back to the present by an appropriate **interest** rate.

If the present value (PV) is to be calculated using a set interest rate (I) acting on just one cash flow many (m) periods from now (Cfm), the formula is:

$$PV = Cfm / (1 + I)^m$$

Note, that Cfm is the future value of that cash flow. So harking back to our future value formula (see **future value** entry), remember that:

$$FV = Cfn \times (1 + I)^P$$

where FV is the value at a specified point in the future of a set of cash flows stretching out from the present to that future point. The set interest rate (I) is acting on an initial cash flow now (Cfn) for a set period (P).

If you look back at the example in the future value entry, you will see that to work out the future value of a $1000 investment today in eight years' time if you earn 9% compound interest, then with Cfn = $1000; I = 9% or 0.09; and P = 8 years.

$$FV = \$1000 \times (1 + 0.09)^8 = \$1000 \times (1.99256) = \$1,992.56$$

Looking again at the present value formula,

$$PV = Cfm / (1 + I)^m$$

it should be clear that Cfm, one cash flow m periods from now, is equivalent to the future value of that cash flow. So using the future value example, where FV = $1,992.56 = Cfm, and still using I = 9% and P = m = 8 years, we find:

$$PV = 1992.56 / (1 + 0.09)^8 = \$1,000.$$

Present value also comes into play in figuring out how much an **annuity** that pays out a set amount of money over many periods is worth today. If an annuity promises to pay at fixed periodic intervals, starting one unit of time out (be it one day, one month, one year, etc.), it is possible to work out its present value.

If the annuity promises to pay over the next m years, 8 in this example, at yearly intervals starting next year, with set payments (PMT) each year of $90, then depending on the interest rate, I, assumed at 9%, it is possible to work out the present value of this annuity (PVA).

$$\mathbf{PVA} = \mathbf{PMT} \times [(1 - \{1/(1 + I)^m\})/I]$$

In our specific example, this works out to:

$$\mathbf{PVA} = 90 \times [(1 - \{1/(1 + 0.09)^8\})/0.09] = \$498.13.$$

Note that because the 9% interest rate is the figure that is used to discount the value of money backward in time, it is appropriately called the 'discount rate'.

In the case when cash flows are not the same in each period, as was the case in our earlier example, the principle still remains the same even if the PVA formula no longer remains valid.

When future cash flows vary, each one must be discounted separately and then summed. This can be done using the first formula we visited in this entry, namely,

$$\mathbf{PV} = \mathbf{Cf}_m/(1 + I)^m$$

and applying it for various 'm' running from 1 to the last period to be considered. The total present value then becomes the sum of all the different PV entries worked out using the basic formula. (See also **investing, future value, IRR** and **NPV**.)

price earnings ratio (multiple)
See **PE, P/E, PER**.

price-sensitive information

Information from either within a **company** or without that will affect its share price as soon as the investing public knows about it.

In the case of price-sensitive information within a company known initially only by company **insider**s, acting in advance of a public announcement for personal benefit is **insider trading**. One example would be the situation where a much hyped up overseas project falls through because of a denial of critical permission from the foreign authorities. This is price-sensitive information that we assume for the sake of this discussion is conveyed to the company's officials in that foreign land on Thursday afternoon.

The people on site immediately phone through with the dire news and inform the **managing director** who then tells the other members of his **board**. For the sake of this illustration we assume some of the **board** members then quietly reduce their holdings in the company on Thursday evening just before trading ends. The official announcement of the failure to secure permission is only made the next Friday morning, and the price of the company's stock takes a beating and heads south. The board members who sold the previous day at what was still a heady price level would have benefited at the expense of unknowing members of the public. Insider trading has taken place on the back of (at that time) undisclosed price-sensitive information.

primary market

When **share**s in a **company** are first offered to the public, the money **investor**s pour into the **IPO** flows directly into the coffers of the company. These investors and the company issuing the shares or the original vendors who are enriched in the process form the primary market. (See **secondary market**.)

prime rate

The interest rate a bank uses as a floor when determining what level of **interest** to charge on loans. The more important and more negotiation 'muscle' a customer has, the closer his loan rate will be to the prime rate. The prime rate is generally above what the bank pays its depositors in interest and below what it charges its loan customers. But in the US, the prime rate specifically refers to the rate banks offer their best and biggest corporate customers. Everybody else gets charged prime plus some mark up. (See also **BLR**.)

principal
A **capital** sum that is invested in the hope of earning **interest** or a **profit**.

private company
A **company** that is privately held by a limited number of **shareholders** and which is not publicly traded on an **exchange**.

private placement
Even if a **company** is listed and therefore traded on an **exchange**, there are times when large **block**s of its **share**s are traded privately, and not through the exchange. This may or may not involve the process of **disintermediation**. If it does, the buyer and seller deal with each other directly. If it does not, a **broker** will still make his cut on the deal but the advantage of a private placement is the maintenance of the prevailing price level. For instance, if Quik Trade Ltd has 10m **issued shares**, and its major shareholder, Mr Dough Roller owns 6m of those, he may wish to sell 1m shares to Ms Fresh Loaf in a private placement. Let's assume the price of Quik Trade's shares is currently $5 a piece with an average daily volume of 200,000 shares. If Dough Roller tried to offload 1m on the same day, the price of Quik Trade would collapse and Dough Roller would not get as much as the current market price of his shares. Similarly, if Fresh Loaf tried to buy 1m shares from the open market, her heavy buying would push the share price **north** and force her to pay far more than if she were merely nibbling. A private placement solves both

problems by allowing a big buyer and a big seller to deal privately and leave the general price level unchanged.

privatisation

The process of reducing the size of government machinery by hiving off traditionally government-run businesses like the power company, the telephone company, the water company, the ports and the post office to the private sector. At its best, privatisation injects new market-driven efficiencies into these industries which should bring prices down. At its worst, privatisation can be misused by crooked politicians as yet another avenue for cronyism. Often increased prices to the consumer suggest a privatisation project is not working as transparently and fairly as it should.

profit

An economic or monetary gain derived from a sound **investment** decision.

Profit and Loss account

P&L, commonly called an income statement in the US.

proxy

One who acts on behalf of another. In the case of voting at an **AGM** or **EGM**, it is possible for a **shareholder** who is indisposed to send a proxy in his stead.

public offering (issue)

An issue of **share**s to the public in either an **IPO** or a subsequent issue.

public offering price

The per share price in an **IPO** or any other **public issue**. The **underwriter** of the issue has a vested interest in making sure the public offering price is not so high that **investor** interest is dampened to the extent that the underwriter is left carrying the bag.

pure discount bond
A **zero coupon bond** with a **nominal value** of one currency unit (eg. $1 or RM1).

put option
An instrument that affords the **holder** the right, but thankfully, given the vagaries of the market, not the obligation to sell the **underlying investment** in question (which he already owns) at a specified price within a set period. If exercised, the **writer** must meet these obligations inherent in allowing the holder the right to sell the actual investment at the price level set by the put option. (See **option** and **call option**.)

put option holder
Owner of a **put option** who believes that the **underlying investment** will fall in price. (See **holder** and **call option holder**.)

Q

quant
A nerdy term for a numbers jock, one who is unusually at home with opaque mathematical formulae. The ideal job for a quant (sometimes derided as a **rocket scientist**) with an **investment** bent would be to run a **quant fund** or to be an extremely numerate **analyst** riveted to his computerised spreadsheet packages.

quant fund
A **mutual fund** run in a highly quantitative **investment** manner. Quant funds are typically run by **quant**s and essentially track the index they are supposed to outperform, and then through mind numbing mathematical legerdemain attempt to pick stocks that will do better than the average thus returning better **returns** for the fund than its **benchmark index**.

quick ratio
acid-test ratio.

quotation

A twinned pair of prices representing the **bid** and **asked** levels of respective buyers and sellers. Generally a buyer will bid a lower price than a seller will ask. Therefore, if the bid price of an asset is $5 and the asked price $5.10, the two numbers form the current quotation. The more **illiquid** an **asset** is, the wider the **spread** between the two levels.

R

R
The single letter code for Ryder Systems, a company listed on the **NYSE**. (See **stock symbol**.)

Rainbow Effect
Although **common stocks** have outperformed every other class of **investment** in the long-term, there is virtually no way of being certain which stock is going to be the next **ten-bagger**. It is identical to never knowing where a rainbow is going to pop up next. The term was coined by Charles L. Fahy in his book *The Streetwise Investor*, co-authored by Sydney Le Blanc (Probus Publishing Co., 1994), to signify the sheer impossibility of figuring out which industry, let alone which stock within it, will be this year's star performer. The point to fathoming the nature of the Rainbow Effect is to drive home the importance of **diversification**.

rally
A surge in price levels of a particular **investment** or of an entire **market**, particularly after a protracted period of lacklustre performance.

RAM
Rating Agency of Malaysia. The country's first private debt rating agency.

ramp
Standard ploy of manipulative trading by **syndicate**s with the aim of creating **speculator** interest. Typically prices are driven high, or 'ramped' up, as speculators rush into the feeding frenzy created by the syndicates. Then, as the price continues to rise on the back of speculative buying, the syndicates gradually off-load their shares at the elevated price levels. Once the syndicates have made their pile, they withdraw from the scene. Very quickly, the entire artifice collapses with many small-time speculators left holding shares that were bought at unjustifiably high prices and that have since returned to levels more in line with the company's **fundamentals**.

Random Walk Theory
Is closely linked to **the Weak Form of the Efficient Market Theory**. In essence both theories maintain that the prices of a **common stock** are independent of each other (that is, independent in time). This means past prices are no help in predicting future prices. The **investment** world is clearly split down the middle (between fundamental and technical-based analysts) as to whether this is true. Proponents of **fundamental research** are more likely to agree with the Random Walk Theory, while **technical analyst**s or **chartist**s most obviously do not.

To quote from Benjamin **Graham** and David Dodd's *Security Analysis* (McGraw-Hill, 1989):

> Compared with all the fortunes made from long-term investing based on in-depth security analysis, the absence of large cumulative additions to wealth from market analysis (**technical analysis**) is a striking commentary. (Chapter 2)

But according Robert D. **Edwards** and John **Magee** in their seminal book, *Technical Analysis of Stock Trends* (John Magee Inc., 1992):

> As a matter of fact, aside from the greenest of newcomers when they first tackle the investment problem, and to whom, in their inexperience, any other point of view is not only irrational but incomprehensible, your pure fundamentalist is a very rare bird. Even those market authorities who pretend to scorn charts and "chartists" utterly, are not oblivious to the "action" chronicled by the ticker tape, nor do they conceal their respect for the **Dow Theory** which, whether they realise it or not, is in its very essence purely technical. (Chapter 1)

Technical practitioners like J. Welles Wilder, Jr, consistently showed their disdain for the Random Walk Theory by building upon Charles **Dow**'s work to further enhance technical analysis. In Wilder's case, his specific formulation of the **RSI** indicator clearly showed his disregard for the Random Walk Theory since his **Relative Strength Index** hinges upon the axiom that yesterday's prices influence today's and both those sets can be used to predict tomorrow's prices with the ultimate aim of laughing all the way to the bank.

Increasingly however modern investment pundits are finding some middle ground between the antagonistic fundamental and technical schools. Also, Malaysian technical guru, Fred KH **Tam** in his *Maximising Stock Market Profit* (Berita Publishing, 1994) draws a distinction between mature and developing markets:

> Unlike the proponents of the Random Walk Theory who claim that price changes are random and unpredictable and as such (it is) pointless to chart past prices, technicians believe that prices do trend and it is essential that technicians accept without any reservations this concept of trend.
>
> (The) Random Walk Theory, based on the Efficient Market Hypothesis, may be applicable to the US markets where all

market sensitive information is almost instantly known to all market participants. In such a scenario, few if any market participants can derive much benefit from privileged information because nothing much is privileged information in an efficient market like the US. But this is not true in many Third World countries where the flow of information is not as transparent. (Chapter 1)

It must also be noted that even if pure fundamentalists tend to whip out the Random Walk Theory whenever the urge to belittle technicians overcomes them, true fundamental analysts believe that superior returns are still achievable by large expenditures of "**brain equity**". That is the primary reason fundamental analysts are paid so much. (See **analyst**.)

But this belief that competent fundamental analysis can indeed reap huge profits is, ironically, itself a major step away from the logical dictates of the Random Walk Theory which pedantically insists that you can't really beat the market, so you might as well not bother.

rating agency
An organisation like Moody's, Standard & Poor or **RAM** which rates the credit worthiness of companies, organisations and even entire countries.

Rating Agency of Malaysia
RAM.

real estate
Landed property as a form of **investment**.

real GDP
GDP in real terms after factoring out the effects of **inflation**. For instance, if a country's real GDP in 1997 is $2 trillion, and its real GDP growth rate is 4% while inflation is 3% for that year, then in

1998 the country's real GDP is 4% more than its 1997 level, but roughly 7% (3% + 4%) more in nominal terms. The compounding effect has been ignored for the purpose of this illustration.

realised loss
As opposed to a **paper loss**, this is an actual loss that has been taken through the **liquidation** of a depreciated **asset**.

realised profit
As opposed to a **paper gain**, this is an actual gain that has been taken through the **liquidation** of an appreciated **asset**. (See **take profit**.)

realised rate of return
A rate of **return** in percentage terms that has actually been realised, as opposed to merely being a rate of return calculated based on **paper profits**. For a **stock**, at any one time, the realised rate of return involves the actual **capital gain** plus all **dividend**s paid in the period of ownership. For a **bond** it is similarly any **capital gain** plus all **coupon** payments. One advantage of regularly milking the gains made in investments and putting the profits to work in other tangible areas is highlighted by the old investment maxim, 'No one ever went broke taking a profit.' (See **Tam**'s rule 'i'.)

recession
A period of economic contraction. It is technically defined as at least two consecutive quarters of negative **GNP** expansion, or in more simple terms six months in which the Gross National Product shrinks.

red ink
Common term for corporate losses. (See **accumulated tax credits**.)

regulators
Public agencies like the **Securities Exchange Commission (SEC)** in the US, the **Monetary Authority of Singapore (MAS)** and the

Securities Commission (SC) in Malaysia, which oversee the practices of listed companies for the common good of the **investment** industry and the protection of minority shareholders.

reinvestment

The act of investing the earned returns, like **dividend**s, on a previous **investment** by buying more of the same. For instance, if you own 10,000 shares of ABC Ltd, currently trading at $5 a share, your present investment is worth $50,000. If ABC's board then declares a $0.10 dividend, you will get $1,000 in dividend income. Ignoring the effect of **taxation** for the purposes of this example, if you believe enough in the future prospects of ABC, you might go down the reinvestment path and use your $1,000 to buy another 200 shares in ABC, thus upping your stake in the company to 10,200 shares.

Note that in this instance your actions have increased your proportional ownership in ABC, which would not have been the case if a **stock dividend** of 20 shares per 1,000 owned had been issued. This incidentally also illustrates the greater benefits generally accruing to a **cash dividend**.

Relative Strength Index

An index widely used in technical analysis developed by J. Welles Wilder, Jr. The RSI formula is:

$$RSI = 100 - \left[\frac{100}{\left\{ 1 + \left(\frac{\text{average upclose value}}{\text{average downclose value}} \right) \right\}} \right]$$

(where an upclose is a closing price higher than the previous one, and a downclose is a closing price lower than the previous corresponding one.)

Generally when the RSI figure is above 70, the market is considered overbought and ready to be sold down, and if the RSI is under 30, the market is deemed oversold and ready to be bought higher.

Reminiscences of a Stock Operator
A book by Edwin Lefevre on Jesse Lauriston **Livermore**, first published in 1923 by George H. Doran and Company, reissued by John Wiley & Sons in 1994.

remisier
A self-employed equities dealer who is attached to a stock broking firm. A remisier cultivates a pool of clients who use him to effect **share** trades. In exchange for this, the remisier retains a portion of the **commission** charged by the broking firm. The downside is the enormous **risk** a remisier takes on whenever he trades for his clients. Until the money is disbursed by the client to pay for a buy trade, for instance, the remisier is held responsible for the sum involved. For example, in Malaysia, remisiers take 40% of the usual 1% broking commission charged by the firms they are attached to. If the remisier buys RM1m worth of stock for a client, he is liable for that full million until the money is paid. In contrast, the commission earned on that deal for the remisier is only RM4,000.

In **bull market**s remisiers can make huge sums of money, but the mark of a sound remisier is whether he can retain most of his supernormal profits when the market heads **south**, as it always eventually will for a season, and his clients get burned. Because if his clients then choose to run out on him, the remisier is responsible for their losses.

Renminbi
The Chinese currency. It is equivalent to the **Yuan**, with the major distinction that the Renminbi is reserved for dealings with foreigners. The idea of having two equivalent currencies, one for domestic use and the other for foreign is to allow the Chinese authorities greater control over precious reserves of hard foreign **currency**. (See **currencies**.)

Repelia VI
Indonesia's current five-year development plan for 1994 to 1998.

research
The utilisation of "**brain equity**" to unearth valuable **investment**s that should be bought, or even overvalued ones that ought to be sold. This is the primary arsenal of the **fundamental analyst** intent on proving the **Efficient Market Theory** wrong. (See **fundamentals**.)

resistance
A term used by **chartist**s to denote a price level above which a **stock** has problems going. (See **support**.)

retained earnings
Also known as **unappropriated profit**, this is the portion of a company's earnings for the year that it keeps within its coffers and does not distribute back to **shareholders** in the form of **dividend**s.

return
Gain from an **investment**. (See **ten-bagger** and **returns**.)

return on assets
ROA. It is worked out in this way:

$$ROA = (net\ profit/total\ assets) \times 100\%$$

return on equity
ROE. It is worked out in this way:

$$ROE = (net\ profit/shareholders'\ equity) \times 100\%$$

return on investment
The overall gain from an **investment** including capital appreciation and income. In the case of a property investment, this would include all rents collected over the life of the investment plus the capital gain on the sale of the property.

returns
See **return on investment**.

Reuters
It is absolutely essential that if you want to pass off as someone in-the-know when it comes to business that you pronounce this wire services' name correctly – *roy-ters*. Under no circumstance deal with a **broker** who mispronounces this essential service that provides useful investment news and live stock price coverage from every major **market** in the world.

reverse takeover
A graphic corporate term to describe what happens when a small **company** swallows a larger one. If this bigger company is a listed one, the smaller one will have effected a **back-door listing**.

reward
A gain in the **investment** game that is earned for taking on **risk**.

RHB
Rashid Hussain Bhd, largest **brokerage** in Southeast Asia, headed by high-powered Malaysian stock broker turned banker Tan Sri Rashid Hussain.

Riel
The Cambodian currency. (See **currencies**.)

Ringgit (RM)
The Malaysian currency. (See **currencies**.)

rights
See **rights issue**.

rights issue

The most obvious way for a company to make a **cash call**. If Cash Strapped Ltd has a paid up capital of $5m, made up of 5m shares each with a **nominal value** of $1, it may be in a quandary if faced with a great opportunity to invest in, perhaps, a timber venture in Kalimantan requiring an additional $10m in funds to purchase a small concession and to upgrade its saw mills. If Cash-Strapped is currently trading at $3 per share, it has a **market capitalisation** of $15m ($3 x 5m). If its **board** decides to raise the needed $10m through a rights issue, it may apply to the **regulators** for permission to have a 1–for–1 rights issue at $2 a rights share.

This means that each **shareholder** will have the right to buy 1 new share at $2 for every share he currently holds. To see if this exercise is worth his while a canny investor cannot merely look at the prevailing market price of $3 and decide that the rights offer price of $2 is so cheap that the offer is attractive. What must be considered is the fact that the 5m new shares will expand Cash Strapped's **equity base**. Generally this will result in a **dilution** of each share's earnings' backing; **EPS** may therefore fall.

What must be calculated is a **theoretical ex-rights price**. This adjusts the current market capitalisation by the new cash flowing into the company's coffers and the resultant rise in the number of shares of the same company. This is how that seemingly daunting task is done.

$$\text{Theoretical ex-rights price} = \frac{[(\text{current number of shares} \times \text{current price}) + (\text{fresh capital injected})]}{\text{new number of shares}}$$

In this example, that works out to

$$= \frac{[(5m \times \$3) + (5m \times \$2)]}{(5m + 5m)}$$
$$= \$2.50$$

Because the rights offer price is $2 and the theoretical ex-rights price is $2.50, there is a 25% **margin of comfort** for the investor planning to take up the rights offer. Also, for the investor not willing or unable to do so, he may consider selling off his stake outright because each of his shares, now valued at $3, should fall to $2.50, after the exercise. (Consider **Fisher's Point 13**.)

Rip van Winkle Effect

In the legend, this character magically fell asleep for decades. This term has been coined by some **investment** writers to refer to the benefits of adopting a **buy and hold** strategy over many, many years because of the equally magical (and extraordinarily profitable) effects of **compounding**.

risk

Investment risk is something that every **investor,** and especially **speculator,** must learn to live with. In the 6th edition of Frederick Amling's textbook, *Investments – An Introduction to Analysis & Management* (Prentice Hall, 1989), there are four explicit forms of investment risk: broad market risk, specific business risk, money rate risk which revolves around the effects shifting interest rates have on **bond** investments, and the ever present **inflation** risk which impacts all of us.

Taking all these into consideration, it is vital, as a general guide for novices of **investment** and all others who value their health, to make sure that you sell down your exposure in risky investments to the point of being able to sleep soundly at night.

General investment risks can also be said to fall into these five categories:

a. Market timing
When you invest at a peak and suddenly find your markets heading south for an indeterminate length of time;

b. Lost opportunity

Even something as seemingly risk-free as investing in fixed deposits can turn out to be a wrong move if you are locked into ones with low interest rates at a time when **monetary tightening** sees **interest rates** ratcheted upward by the authorities.

c. Credit risk

In the case of **junk bond**s, bad times could mean that companies with basement credit ratings justify those profiles by skipping interest payments, or worse, declaring themselves insolvent.

d. Interest-rate risk

While this seems to match the case of (b. Lost opportunity), it really hinges on the inverse relationship between **bond** prices and **interest rates**. If interest rates rise, bond prices fall. Generally, the longer the maturity period of the bond, the greater the price drop.

e. Diversification risk

Too little diversification can result in excessive exposure to the vagaries of specific holdings. Too much diversification could see the sterling performance of your star holdings weighed down by the many other laggards in your basket.

(adapted from *Diversify Your Way to Wealth* by Gerald W. Perritt and Alan Levine, Heinemann Asia, 1994, Chapter 2)

risk averse

Generally, the characteristic of not wanting to take on any **risk** whatsoever. (See **risk profile**.)

But under an assumption in **Modern Portfolio Theory** (see **Modern Portfolio Theory Assumption 2**), being risk averse specifically refers to an investor's sole willingness to take on more risk if greater reward can be expected, and not otherwise. (See **risk-reward ratio**.)

It is therefore vital to ascertain in any reading of **investment**-related literature which of the two meanings is intended.

risk-free asset
Hypothetically deemed to be a short-term US Treasury instrument, therefore a **Treasury bill**, that is supposed to be utterly risk-free because it is backed by the most powerful government in the world. However, at the rate the US twin deficits are escalating, some theoreticians are beginning to question the accuracy of the term.

risk-free rate
The current rate being offered by a **risk-free asset**.

risk loving (seeking)
The characteristic of actively seeking out more **risk** with the intent of making huge profits though the driving force is often not the aim of making more money but the thrill of nearly losing it all, or sometimes actually doing so. (See **risk profile**.)

risk neutral
The characteristic of being willing to take on moderate risk for moderate gains. (See **risk profile**.)

risk premium
The additional return above the **risk-free rate** expected by an **investor** from an **investment** to make up for his willingness to exercise his **risk tolerance**.

risk profile
An investor's psychological make-up that determines whether he is **risk averse**, **risk neutral** or **risk loving**.

risk-reward ratio
A mathematical determination of the attractiveness of an **investment**. Usually the higher the risk, the greater the possible reward. A **risk loving** person would seek out investments with a high risk-reward ratio like futures trading, while a **risk averse** one would probably settle for putting money in the bank. In a sense

both are still at risk, since the risk lover stands to lose his capital (and his shirt) while the risk hater might lose out on the purchasing power of his money through the inevitable eroding action of **inflation**. (See **beta** and **SML**.)

risk to holder
Degree of risk the holder of an option assumes by virtue of owning it. Explicitly, the **holder** of any **option** is only putting at **risk** the amount of money he paid for that **option**, called its **premium**. (See **risk to writer**.)

risk to writer
Degree of risk the writer of an option assumes by writing it in the first place. The **writer** of an **option** puts at **risk** either the price of an offsetting **option** (see **writer of a covered option**) or the entire current market price of the option (see **writer of a naked option**), depending on what type of option he writes.

risk tolerance
The amount of **risk** that an **investor** is willing to subject himself to with the aim of making a certain amount of money, his **reward**. (See **risk-reward ratio**.)

ROA
return on assets.

rocket scientist
Apart from a NASA or ESA employee, also a **quant**.

ROE
return on equity.

ROI
return on investment.

round lot
An American term for **board lot**.

RSI
Relative Strength Index.

Rule of 72
An immensely useful and fun way of working out how long it will take to double an **investment** given a steady percentage return. (See **CAGR**). If you put $1000 in the bank at 3% a year, the Rule of 72 tells you it will take roughly 24 years to have **compound interest** work to double your money to $2000. If the bank pays 8% instead, the Rule of 72 tells you it will take only 9 years to double your money. To apply the rule simply take the number 72 and divide it by the interest rate in percentage terms. In our two examples that works out to $72/3 = 24$ and $72/8 = 9$.

Alternatively if you want to double your money in 4 years, then seek out an investment that will pay $72/4 = 18\%$ a year. This 18% represents the CAGR required to give you that return. Just to check, consider the pleasant situation of having $1m at Year 0. If you plonk that money into an investment that **yield**s a consistent 18%, or at least averages out to 18% over the four-year period in question, then at the end of Year 1 you will have $1.18m, Year 2 = 1.39m, Year 3 = $1.64m, Year 4 = $1.94m, pretty close to the $2m doubling mark.

Rupee
The name of the currency of both India and Pakistan. Although distinct currencies, they tend to trade almost at parity. (See **currencies**.)

Rupiah
The Indonesian currency. (See **currencies**.)

S

S
The single letter code for Sears, a company listed on the **NYSE**. (See **stock symbol**.)

SAF
Scudder New Asia Fund.

safe investment
One that carries with it a low risk of loss. In **stock** terms it would be a **company** with a **beta** well below 1.0. However, it must always be realised that due to the usual correlation between **risk** and **reward** (see **risk-reward ratio**) if too little risk is taken on, there may be insufficient reward ensuing to compensate for **inflation**. So in that sense the concept of a single safe investment is suspect. Those who covet genuine safety would be well advised to follow the path of **diversification**.

'sai lang'
In Malaysia, a term in the Chinese Hokkien dialect adopted by market players to describe the hard core gamblers willing to risk everything on a single, speculative stock.

sales per dollar (or local currency like RM, rupiah, baht or peso) of common stock
Is a yardstick occasionally looked at by a **financial analyst**. There is a school of thought (to which Kenneth L. Fisher, the son of Philip A. **Fisher**, belongs) that believes you should not buy a **company** whose **share**s are trading at a level above its sales or turnover per share. (See **sales per share**.)

sales per share
Total turnover for the year / **weighted average number of common shares** outstanding that year

samurai bond
A **bond** issued by non-Japanese entities denominated in **Yen** for the ease of Japanese investors. (See **yankee bond**.)

savvy
Term often used in the financial press to describe a real smart investor or businessman. Particularly important trait to have so as to identify cases of **window dressing**.

SC
Securities Commission.

scrip
In countries where fully **scripless trading** has not taken root yet, the share certificates are pieces of paper that denote ownership of **common equity**. The term for these valuable bits of paper is scrip.

scripless trading
Computerised stock trading that has done away with the need for **scrip** in some countries.

Scudder New Asia Fund

Commonly denoted as **SAF**. This **closed-end fund** is listed on the **NYSE** and was launched in June 1987 by Scudder, Stevens & Clark. Its stated investment objectives are to ride on the long-term capital growth of companies throughout Asia. It does however, concentrate much of its resources in ferreting out sound investments among the minnows of corporate Japan. Price and **NAV** data on **SAF** are readily found in the **AWSJ**. (See **mutual funds**.)

SEC

Securities and Exchange Commission.

secondary market

After the shares of a company are listed on an exchange, the trading subsequent to the IPO is carried out in the secondary market. It is called this because although much money changes hands in the process of the ongoing buying and selling, none of that money goes into the coffers to the company whose shares are being traded. This is in contrast to the **primary market**. (See **IPO**.)

sector

An industry category such as banks, property, trading or utilities.

sector allocation

The division of **investment** funds between different industries of an economy. For instance, if a fund has a country allocation that requires 35% of its money be pumped into the Philippines market, it will then need to figure out how to split that 35% of its total resources among the many industrial sectors of the country. It might choose to put 40% in bank stocks, 30% in property stocks and 30% in utilities. If so, that mix would be its method of sector allocation within that country.

securities
Investment instruments like **bond**s and **stock**s that represent securitised claims on **asset**s like an **IOU** or a **company**'s business.

Securities and Exchange Commission
The federal agency that oversees **securities** trading in the US. Also the equivalent Thai body.

Securities Commission
The statutory body that oversees **securities** trading in Malaysia.

Securities Exchange of Thailand
Thailand's **bourse**, commonly abbreviated to **SET**. (See **SET Index**.)

security analysis
The specific facet of financial analysis that ferrets out, scrutinises, and then attempts to qualitatively and quantitatively assess the **investment** worthiness of individual securities. (See **fundamental analysis**.)

Security Analysis
The seminal book by Benjamin **Graham** and David Dodd, both at one time of New York's Columbia University, first published in 1934, and now in its Fifth Edition. The impact of this book has been far reaching. Its very title has been taken as the generic name (see above) for this vital investment research discipline.

Both Graham and Dodd were so highly regarded by the greatest modern day investor, Warren **Buffett**, that while licking his wounds after being rejected by Harvard Business School, Buffett wrote to a friend:

> To tell you the truth, I was kind of snowed when I heard from Harvard. Presently I am waiting for an application blank from Columbia. They have a pretty good finance department there;

at least they have a couple of hot shots in Graham and Dodd that teach common stock valuation.

(Buffett – The Making of an American Capitalist by Roger Lowenstein, Weidenfeld & Nicolson, 1996, p. 35)

Security Market Line
Commonly abbreviated to SML. It is a straight line relationship between expected **return** and **risk** as measured by **beta**. (See **risk-reward ratio**.)

sell
To dispose of a **stock, bond** or any other **asset**. When an **investment analyst** makes a sell recommendation he expects the **investment** to underperform its **benchmark index**.

Semistrong Form Efficiency
The type of price efficiency inherent in an arena exhibiting the **Semistrong Form of the Efficient Market Theory**.

Semistrong Form of the Efficient Market Theory
States that all publicly available information is always reflected in the market price of common stocks. The basic premise for this is that the flow of information concerning individual stocks, industries, the market and the economy is a constant flood resulting in a rapid set of price corrections. (See **Efficient Market Theory** and **Semistrong Form Efficiency**.)

One failing of the Semistrong Form of the EMT is that a quick price correction does not necessarily result in an accurate readjustment – either in direction or quantum. So much so, Graham and Dodd's *Security Analysis* (McGraw-Hill, 1989, Fifth Edition) insists:

> In essence, there are extramarket returns from analysts' greater diligence and superior understanding which are independent of the timing or breadth of distribution of the information. The

trained, knowledgeable analyst can, and frequently does, interpret information with materially better judgment than that expressed by the consensus in the marketplace. To the extent that this occurs, the semistrong form of market efficiency has not been validated. (Chapter 2)

senior debt
Long-term debt that is repayable after 12 months. (See **subordinate debt**.)

Sensitive Index
See **Bombay Sensitive Index**.

Sensitive Price Index
A secondary index of the Colombo Stock Exchange. (See also **All Shares Price Index**.)

series of options
Options falling in the same class which also have an identical **exercise price** and **expiration date**.

SES
Stock Exchange of Singapore. (See **STII** and **DBS 50**.)

SESDAQ
Stock Exchange of Singapore Dealing and Automated Quotation System. Introduced in February 1987 as a junior exchange to the **SES**.

SET
Securities Exchange of Thailand.

SET Index
The **benchmark index** for the **Securities Exchange of Thailand**.

Seven Cures for a Lean Purse
George Samuel **Clason**'s character **Arkad** in the financial classic **The Richest Man in Babylon** lists these pointers to combat personal poverty. (See **Arkad's Cure 1** to **7 for a Lean Purse**.)

Seventh Malaysia Plan
Malaysia's current five-year development plan for 1996 to 2000.

SGF
Singapore Fund.

Shanghai A Share
An index of stocks reserved for local investors of the **Shanghai Securities Exchange**. (See also **Dow Jones Shanghai** and **Class A**.)

Shanghai B Share
An index of hard currency stocks officially reserved for foreign investors of the **Shanghai Securities Exchange**. However, a recent article in the **Far Eastern Economic Review** ('Battle of the Bourses', September 5, 1996) suggests that about 40–50% of B Share activity involved Chinese domestic participation. (See also **Dow Jones Shanghai** and **Class B**.)

Shanghai Securities Exchange
China's first bourse in modern times, started in December 1990. It is generally seen to be less progressive than its sister bourse in Shenzen. (See **Shenzen Securities Exchange**.)

share
Traditionally a piece of paper (now more usually its electronic equivalent) that represents proportional ownership in a company. If company Small Fry Pte Ltd has four shares issued, each share denotes 25% **equity** in the company. (See **common stock**.)

share price appreciation
What all **investors** want and **bulls** expect. Denoted either in absolute **currency** terms or a percentage. For instance, if a stock you buy at $4 rises to $6, the share price appreciation is $2 or 50% (= {6 − 4}/ 4} x 100%).

share price depreciation
What all **investors** do not want but **bears** expect. Denoted either in absolute **currency** terms or a percentage. No example is needed as everyone who has ever gone into the market knows, there will always be share price depreciation at some time, especially on days that **Mr Market** feels down in the dumps.

shareholders
The legal owners of a company. The extent of their ownership is proportional to the number of **shares** they own relative to the company's **paid up capital**. If a shareholder owns 1,000 shares in a company with a paid up capital made up of 1m shares, he owns exactly one-thousandth of that company.

There are generally two categories of shareholders, major ones who control enough **stock** to justify **board** positions (usually more than 20% of the company) and minority ones who generally can only express their opinions during the voting sessions during **AGM**s and **EGM**s.

shareholders' equity
Because a **company** is owned by all its **shareholders**, the company's **net worth** is equivalent to the shareholders' equity. It is also equal to the **common equity** of a company plus any reserves plus all **retained earnings** over the years.

share split
See **stock split**.

shell company
A **company** that has no significant business to speak off and is therefore nothing more than an incorporated shell. Its primary attractiveness then would be as a target for a **reverse takeover**.

Shenzen A Share
An index of stocks reserved for local investors of the **Shenzen Securities Exchange**. (See also **Dow Jones Shenzen** and **Class A**.)

Shenzen B Share
An index of hard currency stocks officially reserved for foreign investors of the **Shenzen Securities Exchange**. However, a recent article in the **Far Eastern Economic Review** ('Battle of the Bourses', September 5, 1996) suggests that about 70–80% of B Share activity involved Chinese domestic participation. (See also **Dow Jones Shenzen** and **Class B**.)

Shenzen Securities Exchange
China's second bourse in modern times, started in April 1991. It is generally seen as the more progressive of the two Chinese bourses, primarily due to Shenzen's Vice-Mayor **Wu Jiesi**. (See **Shanghai Securities Exchange**.)

short
In its most unadorned sense to sell that which you don't have with a view to making a covering purchase later to balance things out. Those who go short with a view to profit expect a downward price trend.

short position (in an option)
Being **short** in options. It is a **market** position set up by the sale of one option without a balancing purchase being made at that point.

short seller
A vendor who indulges in **short selling**.

short selling
Selling an **asset** you do not have in the hope of effecting a buy-back later at a lower price. In covered short selling, the seller borrows shares from his broker to sell first with a view to make his repayment with subsequently purchased shares. Predictably, a **bear** might consider short selling a stock.

short squeeze
When many short sellers start to buy an **asset** they earlier sold, their buying causes the price to rise thus squeezing the gain they would have made if there were fewer of their number. This is part of the **market**'s self-correcting mechanism when, for instance, a stock with strong fundamentals is inappropriately sold. (See **supply and demand**.)

SIMEX
Singapore International Monetary Exchange. (Also see **stock index futures contract** and **Leeson, Nick**.)

simple interest
As opposed to the more attractive **compound interest** (assuming you are investing money and not borrowing it), simple interest only sees the initial **principal** sum continue to earn interest in each period.

The interest earned in previous periods is not added to the principal to increase the amount of interest earned in subsequent time slices.

Singapore Fund
Commonly denoted as **SGF**. This **closed-end fund** is listed on the **NYSE** and was launched in July 1990 by DBS Asset Management Pte Ltd. Its stated investment objectives are to ride on the long-term capital growth of companies in Singapore though it does dabble in Malaysian stocks. Price and **NAV** data on **SGF** are readily found in the **AWSJ**. (See **mutual funds**.)

SITIC
Shanghai International Trust & Investment Corporation. One of its funds, the **YRDF**, is the first in China to channel foreign-raised capital in Chinese **Class A shares**.

SML
Security Market Line.

soft loan
An extremely low interest loan, well below current market interest rates, usually extended to corporations that are involved in huge infrastructure projects. Many soft loans are made to the developing world by multilateral organisations like the **World Bank** and the **IMF**.

south
Falling prices in a **market**. As in 'prices head south'.

S&P
The common abbreviation for the Standard and Poor's Corporation based in New York City and owned by McGraw-Hill.

S&P 500
Standard and Poor's 500 Index which incorporates 500 US stocks, made up of 400 industrial companies, 40 financial ones, 40 utilities and 20 transportation companies. This weighted **index** is the **benchmark index** used by **institutional investor**s in the US.

speculating
Indulging in the act of **speculation**.

speculation
Short-term indulging in the **stock market**, property sector or other **investment** areas in the hope of making one or several speedy

killings. The **speculator** is a breed apart and distinct from a true **investor**.

While a certain degree of speculation is needed to keep markets alive and hopping, too much of it can be detrimental to the overall good of an economy. According to English economist, John Maynard Keynes:

> Speculators may do no harm as bubbles on a steady stream of enterprise. But the position is serious when enterprise becomes the bubble on a whirlpool of speculation. When the capital development of the country becomes a by-product of the activities of a casino, the job is likely to be ill-done.
>
> (*The General Theory of Employment, Interest and Money, Book 4*, Harcourt Brace, 1936)

speculative gains
Money made through **speculation** as opposed to **investing**.

speculative stock
A stock that may not have strong **fundamentals** but yet is attractive to the **speculator** because of rumours of profitable changes.

speculator
One who habitually indulges in the dangerous game of **speculation**. The most famous speculator of all was Jesse Lauriston **Livermore**. Unlike the bona fide investor, a **speculator** is willing to gamble his future wealth on the chance of making a big killing quickly. (See **ramp** and **syndicate**.)

split
See **stock split**.

spot market
In **futures**, the current market. In commodities, the cash market for immediate physical delivery.

spot price
The current price of an **investment** or **asset** in the **spot market**.

spread
As the term itself suggests, it signifies a difference. In this instance between an **asked** price (by a seller, and therefore a higher one) and a bid price (by a buyer, therefore lower). So,

spread = asked − bid

stag
Anyone who applies for **IPO** shares with the aim of selling them immediately for a quick gain. Therefore a stag obviously does not adopt a **buy and hold strategy**.

stagflation
The sad situation where an economy is in **depression** and therefore stagnating, yet also undergoes high **inflation**. The term is a marriage of *stag*nation and in*flation*.

stale bull
A one-time **bull** who gets caught with too many shares when the **market** turns **south** and generally gets fed up with the market. He then looks to sell as soon as his stocks again reach his purchase levels. The combined selling of many stale bulls can create a **resistance** level and temporarily put the brakes on an eventual strong market recovery.

standard deviation
A statistical measure of dispersion that allows you to figure out which numbers in a set of data fall near the mean and which fall far from it. In a **bell curve**, also called a **normal distribution curve** or **Gaussian distribution**, 34.13% of the total area resides between the middle of the normal curve and one standard deviation to its right. Because of the perfect symmetry of the normal curve, which gives it its

alternative name, the bell curve, obviously 68.26% of the total area lies within one standard deviation of the mean, 34.13% on each side.

In **investment** terms, this usually means that if you look at a large enough universe of stocks, or any other instruments, you will be able to work out the average return from those investments. That would be your mean. If you use a fancy calculator you should be able to quickly work out the standard deviation of your universe. For argument's sake, if your universe of stocks is 500, you might find that in any one-year period the average return on that universe was 15%. Also let's assume your high tech calculator has thrown out 5% as the standard deviation. This means that 68.26% of your stocks, or 341 fall within one standard deviation of the average return. Looked at another way, 341 stocks were about average with returns running from (15 - 5)% to (15 + 5)%, or 10% to 20%. Furthermore, the really high-flyers and the real **dog**s fall outside of one standard deviation of the mean. You'll easily realise that 15.87% of all the stocks were good performers and an equal proportion were dogs.

standard normal distribution
A **normal distribution curve** that has been scaled such that the total area under it is equal to one square unit.

STII
Straits Times Industrial Index, the **benchmark index** of the **SES** for Singapore-based fund managers who nonetheless also keep a nervous eye on how the **DBS 50** is performing.

stock
Except in the case of **Noah** and others interested in husbandry, this refers to ownership **shares** in a company.

stock broker
A **dealer** or **broker** in **equities**.

stock dividend

A **dividend** paid in **stock**, as opposed to a **cash dividend**. The only problem with a stock dividend is that because every other shareholder gets it in the proportion of his holdings, there is no change at all in proportional ownership. If everything else stays the same, the company will warrant exactly the same market capitalisation after the declaration of the stock dividend as before. This means that more shares are divided up into the same business pie. Theoretically, at least then, the stock price should fall some to compensate for the dilution of **earnings** backing each **share**. The effect is somewhat similar to a **bonus issue**.

stock exchange

An exchange like the **NYSE**, **SES**, **KLSE** or **SET** where **equities** are traded.

Stock Exchange of Singapore Dealing and Automated Quotation System
SESDAQ.

stock index
See **index**.

stock index futures contract

A futures contract, like the one traded on **KLOFFE** based on the **KLSE CI**, or on **SIMEX** on the **Nikkei-225**, that allows an investor to **hedge** or speculate on the direction of the overall market. This is the foundational instrument of **PI**.

stock market

A **bourse** like the **NYSE**, **KLSE** and **SES** on which **equities** are traded.

stock split

Unlike a bonus issue that is financed out of a company's coffers, a stock split merely sees each issued share split to make the stock more accessible to investors. If the **nominal value** of a share is $1, after a 1–for–1 split, the most common kind, the nominal value is $0.50, and the **paid up capital** of the **company** is unchanged. However, because of the greater affordability of individual shares, they might attract some additional retail buying. If this occurs the price might rise above the theoretical value. If that happens, market capitalisation rises.

stock symbol

Also merely called the **symbol**. It is the unique letter sequence that distinguishes one listed stock from another. For instance the **Reuters** stock symbol for Malaysian power utility Tenaga Nasional is TENA.KL. On the **New York Stock Exchange**, Warren **Buffett**'s flagship **Berkshire Hathaway**'s A shares have the stock symbol BRKA, while Sears' is just the single letter 'S'.

stop-loss

An order you would give your **broker**, **dealer** or **remisier** to make sure that an **investment** you buy will be automatically sold if it falls below a certain price level. For instance, if a **stock**, Southerly Inclinations Ltd is bought at $23 a share, the buyer may choose to put in a stop-loss order at $21 to protect his downside in case his **tipster** is wrong, as usual.

straight line depreciation

The most common form of **depreciation** used by companies. If an **asset** costs $50m and has a useful life of 10 years, straight line depreciation would see an equal amount, $5m, being written off in the **profit and loss account** of each of the ensuing 10 years, until the asset is fully depreciated.

strike price
The price at which an **option holder** can, if he so chooses depending on market conditions and his own financial health, buy (or sell) the underlying stock in exercising a **call** (or **put**) option. Also called the **exercise price**.

Strong Form Efficiency
The type of price efficiency inherent in an arena exhibiting the **Strong Form of the Efficient Market Theory**.

Strong Form of the Efficient Market Theory
States that the price of stocks or any other securitised **investment** fully reflects all possible information that can be known.

Therefore, in-depth ferreting by **analyst**s cannot produce results markedly better than that of the overall market as it is their own work which partly helps all available information to come to roost everywhere. (See **Efficient Market Theory** and **Strong Form Efficiency**.)

strong market
A sustained rising market where buyers are aggressively buying while sellers are slow to offload in the hope of receiving ever higher prices. (See **bull market**.)

submarine order
In a time of great **market** disarray some people tempted to take advantage of the situation may put in a **buy** order for a **stock** well below its last closed price. For instance, if ABC Ltd closed at $30 on Friday evening, and if war is declared again in the Gulf over the weekend, a submarine order placed on Monday morning might be to **bid** on the stock for $15. The intention is to panic sellers into offloading the stock to the one making the order, at that price, in fear.

183

When a submarine order works it usually results in an eventual gain for the buyer when the market realises it's been conned and that ABC's price level should be much higher.

subordinate debt
Another term for short-term debt which must be repaid in the next 12 months, in contrast to **senior debt**.

subsidiary
A company more than half-owned (at least 50% + 1 **share**) by a **parent company** above it in the group hierarchy. (See **associate**.)

sunset industry
An industry, like rubber in Malaysia or textiles in the US, that is on a seemingly irreversible national decline. The shifting competitive advantage of nations generally tends to result in an industry turning sunset in one country and rising in another.

supply and demand
See **demand and supply** and **market forces**.

support
A term used by **chartists** to denote a price level which a **stock** has problems going below. (See **resistance**.)

sustainable growth rate
An **EPS** growth rate that a **company** is capable of maintaining over the next four to ten years.

symbol
stock symbol.

symmetric hedging strategy
An egalitarian hedging strategy that eliminates the possibility of loss, but in the process also eliminates the possibility of gain. (See **asymmetric hedging strategy**.)

syndicate
An informal grouping of a few or many individuals who have the financial muscle to manipulate a **stock**. The syndicate's aim is to generate interest in a particular company's stock, and to fuel the rumours with carefully patterned buying and selling activity between its members. As the stock's price rises, the syndicates cash out leaving unwary speculators holding shares bought at too high a price. (See **ramp** and **speculator**.)

syndicated loan
Since banks are generally **risk averse**, not just in the way they invest their own funds but especially in the way they lend **money** out, they usually like to spread the **risk** of a large loan out with other banks. When a group of such banks gets together for the common purpose of extending a single huge loan, the group would be a **syndicate** of banks and the loan obviously a **syndicated loan**. A syndicate of banks is not to be confused with a **syndicate** of stock manipulators.

T

T
The single letter code for AT&T, a company listed on the **NYSE**. (See **stock symbol**.)

Taiwan Fund
Commonly denoted as **TWN**. This **closed-end fund** is listed on the **NYSE** and was launched in December 1986 by China Securities Investment Trust Corporation. Its stated investment objectives are to ride on the long-term capital growth of Taiwanese companies. Price and **NAV** data on **TWN** are readily found in the **AWSJ**. (See **mutual funds**.)

Taiwan Stock Exchange
The **bourse** of Taiwan Republic of China, commonly abbreviated to **TSE**. It began life on February 9, 1962, and unlike most exchanges is not owned by the broking firms that do business on it. It is government-owned through various corporate entities.

Taka
The Bangladeshi currency. (See **currencies**.)

take-or-pay basis

The foundation for a contract that requires a buyer to take delivery of a set quantity of goods from the vendor. Should the buyer choose not to do so, he still needs to pay for that amount. Such contracts are common in the gas and electricity businesses. In Malaysia, for instance, YTL Power, the country's first **IPP** negotiated a power uptake contract on a take-or-pay basis with the main power utility, Tenaga Nasional Bhd.

takeover

As its name suggests, a takeover is quite literally the situation where one company takes over control of another. This is done through the accumulation or one-time purchase of a controlling **block** of shares. While gaining control of 50% of the paid up capital plus 1 share, would automatically grant one company control of another, an effective takeover can also be done with as little as 20% of a company, if the rest of the shareholding is fragmented. Takeovers can be friendly or hostile. A friendly one is deemed beneficial to all parties, especially the enriched, outgoing major shareholders. In hostile takeover attempts, it possible that the predator is merely looking to **greenmail** the major shareholders of the target company. In some hostile takeover situations the desperate defensive machinations of shareholders take on fancy names like 'scorched earth tactics' and 'poison pill' manoeuvres.

take profit

Turning a **paper profit** into a **realised profit**.

Tam, Fred KH

A Malaysian **fund manager** generally viewed as the country's guru of **technical analysis**. Author of *Maximising Stock Market Profit* (Berita Publishing, 1994) and *Understanding KLCI Stock Index Futures* (Times Editions, 1996). The second book outlines 10 rules of successful futures trading, 9 of which revolve around sound money management. The 10 are:

a. Use money that you can afford to lose.
b. Don't overtrade.
c. Cut your losses short, let your profits run.
d. If you get into a losing streak, take a breather.
e. Build a pyramid when adding to a profitable trade – if you make money by being **long** before the market starts to rise, when it does do so, do not double up on your exposure. For instance, if you are 20 contracts long initially, the next addition should be 10 contracts, and the one after 5, and so on. This is to protect your gains should there be a sudden reversal.
f. Never add to a losing position.
g. Don't risk your entire capital on one trade. A similar view is espoused by Victor Sperandeo dubbed by Barron's as the 'ultimate Wall Street pro'. In his book, *Trader Vic II - Principles of Professional Speculation* (John Wiley & Sons, 1994), he writes:

> ... in the early stages of a new accounting period, I risk only a small fraction, at most 2 or 3 percent, of available capital in any position, regardless of the reward potential. (p. 5)

h. Never meet margin calls. This does not mean being dishonest but rather having the strength to admit you were wrong, take a small loss and survive to fight another day. The story of Barings and Nick **Leeson** may have been different if the 'Rogue Trader' had heeded this advice.
i. Remove profits from your account. When money is made in the market, extract some of it and put it into hard assets like real estate or low risk instruments like fixed deposit accounts.
j. Have a game plan. Know your destination so that you will know when you arrive and what you are supposed to do when you're there.

taxation

A fact of life, whether you are an individual or a corporation. According to Benjamin Franklin, only two things are ever for certain, death and taxes. One good thing about corporate taxation though is the ability a company has to carry forward losses from previous years to offset the tax charge in a year when it makes a profit. (See **accumulated tax credits** and **tax credits**.)

tax credits

General benefits accruing to companies which can be used to offset **taxation** charges. These include losses made in previous years (for an example see **accumulated tax losses**) as well as specific tax breaks arising from reinvestment allowances and a country's policy of awarding pioneer status to companies in special industries.

T-bill
Treasury bill.

TC
Thai Capital Fund.

technical analysis

The *yang* to the *yin* of **fundamental analysis**. The technical analyst or **chartist** looks at historical price and trading volume charts, as well as **moving average**s, to determine **buy** and **sell** signals.

According to Robert D. Edwards and John Magee, technical analysis:

> ... refers to the study of the action of the market itself as opposed to the study of the goods in which the market deals. Technical analysis is the science of recording, usually in graphic form, the actual history of trading (price changes, volume transactions, etc.) in a certain stock or in 'the averages' and then deducing from that pictured history the probable future trend.

> (*Technical Analysis*, John Magee Inc., 1992, Chapter 1)

As such, it is possible that a proponent of technical analysis is entirely comfortable buying a company on the basis of the charts with no clue as to what the company's fundamental business is about. Such an approach is anathema to those intuitively more comfortable with fundamental analysis.

Some middle of the road pundits however use fundamental analysis to identify good stocks to buy and technical analysis to tell them when exactly to do that buying. Just to show that it takes all kinds to make the investment world go around, there are then hordes of others who are convinced it is impossible to time a market and therefore a **passive investment strategy** like **buy and hold** is the best avenue to permanent riches. Such people would not give chartists like Malaysia's Fred **Tam**, for instance, the time of day. (See **Efficient Market Theory**.)

Technical Analysis of Stock Trends
The basic textbook of **technical analysis** co-authored by Robert D. **Edwards** and John **Magee**.

technical analyst
A **chartist** who utilises **technical analysis** to predict **market** and specific **stock** movements.

technical rally
A strengthening of a **market** or a particular **stock** for no reason that can be attributed to fundamentals. A technical analyst would subscribe to the belief that such a boost or rally is due purely to **technicals**.

technicals
Historical price and volume data used by the **technical analyst** to predict **stock** and **market** movements independent of **fundamentals**.

TEMF
Templeton Emerging Markets Fund.

Templeton Emerging Markets Fund
Commonly denoted as **TEMF** or just EMF. This **closed-end fund** is listed on the **NYSE** and was launched in February 1987 by Templeton, Galbraith & Hansberger. Its stated investment objectives are to ride on the long-term capital growth of companies throughout the world. It allocates assets across continents the way most other international funds do for a range of countries. Price and **NAV** data on **TEMF** are readily found in the **AWSJ**. (See **mutual funds**.)

ten-bagger
The dream of every **investor** is to find the next ten-bagger (or better still, twelve-bagger or twenty-bagger). If you **invest** in a **stock** at $2 a share, and it then appreciates ten-fold to $20, you are the happy owner of a ten-bagger. In percentage terms, a two-bagger **yield**s a 100% **return**, a three-bagger 200%, a ten-bagger 900% return, and so on.

term structure of interest rates
Same as **yield curve**.

Thai Capital Fund
Commonly denoted as **TC**. This **closed-end fund** is listed on the **NYSE** and was launched in May 1990 by The Mutual Fund Company Ltd. Like **TTF**, its stated investment objectives are to ride on the long-term capital growth of Thai companies. Price and **NAV** data on **SAF** are readily found in the **AWSJ**. (See **mutual funds**.)

Thai Fund
Commonly denoted as **TTF**. This **closed-end fund** is listed on the **NYSE** and was launched in February 1988 by The Mutual Fund Company Ltd and Morgan Stanley Asset Management. Like **TC**, its stated investment objectives are to ride on the long-term capital growth of Thai companies. Price and **NAV** data on **TTF** are readily found in the **AWSJ**. (See **mutual funds**.)

Thailand Stock Exchange
Informal name for the **Securities Exchange of Thailand**.

Thailand Stock Exchange Index
Informal designation for the **SET Index**.

The Asian Wall Street Journal
The **AWSJ**.

The Fed
The US' **Federal Reserve System**. Although its name suggests that it is a solely American entity, the truth is more encompassing. Decisions affecting US interest rates, for instance, emanating from the Fed can have direct repercussions on stock prices in the US. By extension, because the NYSE leads the world, the performance of bourses across the planet are to some extent all dependent upon it.

The Massachusetts Investors Trust
The world's first **mutual fund** company started in Boston, Massachusetts, USA, in 1924. Today it is called State Street Research.

The Motley Fool
The supremely successful **investment** club on the **Internet**, founded by David and Tom **Gardner**.

theoretical ex-rights price
See **rights issue** for details and an example. This calculated price level is a mathematical attempt to assess the impact of a rights issue and the ensuing cash inflow and **equity base** expansion on a share's price.

$$\text{Theoretical ex-rights price} = \frac{[\{(\text{current number of shares}) \times (\text{current price})\} + \{\text{fresh capital injected}\}]}{\text{new number of shares}}$$

theoretical value of a right

If a stock is currently trading without rights (**ex**-rights, meaning the issue of rights has already taken place) it is possible to work out mathematically what that right should be worth.

For instance, let us once again look at the case of Cash-Strapped Ltd we were introduced to under the **rights issue** entry.

To recap, Cash-Strapped Ltd has a paid up capital of $5m, made up of 5m shares each with a **nominal value** of $1. It needs $10m more in funds to invest in a timber venture. It decides to make a 1-for-1 rights issue at a subscription price of $2 a rights share.

The **cum**-rights (before the rights issue takes place) price of each Cash-Strapped share is $3, and the ex-rights price is $2.50.

In our original case the theoretical value of a right (TVoaR) is:

$$\text{TVoaR} = \frac{\text{(Market price} - \text{Subscription price)}}{\text{Number of shares needed to get one rights share}}$$

$$= (2.50 - 2)/1$$

$$= \$0.50$$

If Cash-Strapped decides it is able to generate $2m internally and only needs to raise $8m, it could opt for a 4-for-5 rights issue at $2 to raise $8m instead, we can then recalculate the theoretical ex-rights price:

$$\text{Theoretical ex-rights price} = \frac{\{(\text{current number of shares} \times \text{current price}) + (\text{fresh capital injected})\}}{\text{new number of shares}}$$

$$= \frac{\{(5m \times 3) + (8m)\}}{(5m + 4m)}$$

$$= \$2.56$$

… then, the theoretical value of a right is:

$$\text{TVoaR} = \frac{\text{(Market price} - \text{Subscription price)}}{\text{Number of shares needed to get one rights share}}$$

$$= (2.56 - 2)/(5/4)$$
$$= \$0.45$$

In practical terms however, if the rights of a company are traded, then their value moves in tandem with the mother share in a roughly linear fashion. For instance, in the last example if the market price of the mother share jumps $1 above our calculated theoretical ex-rights price, our formula suggests that the theoretical value of one right = (3.56 − 2)/(5/4) = $1.25, only $0.80 (and not $1) above its TVoaR when the market price of the mother share moved up $1. However, note that in terms of percentage appreciation, the rights are more attractive. When the mother share moved 39% up from $2.56 to $3.56, the rights jumped 178% from $0.45 to $1.25.

The Richest Man in Babylon
A financial inspirational classic by George Samuel **Clason** made up of a series of Babylonian parables about thrift and sound investment principles. The richest man whose wisdom forms the pivot of the book is **Arkad**. Some of these are listed under the **Seven Cures for a Lean Purse** and the **Five Laws of Gold**.

The Wall Street Journal
America's premier business newspaper. The parent publication of the **Asian Wall Street Journal (AWSJ**.)

thin market
A market undergoing a period of low **volume**.

tight market
A market trading in such a way that its **benchmark index** only moves within an extremely **tight range**.

tight range
Little or no movement in prices or an **index**.

time
The ultimate friend of an **investor** because of the effects of **compounding**. And the nemesis of a debtor, for the same reason.

time value
For an **option**, the time value represents the difference between its overall **premium** and its **intrinsic value**. At any fixed price level, the time value of an option falls until it hits zero, zip, nada, upon **expiration**. This inexorable decline in time value makes an **option** a prime example of a **wasting asset**.

time value of money
Since money in your hands today can earn more money tomorrow through the power of **compounding**, it is intuitively obvious that $100 given to you today is worth more than $100 given to you tomorrow. For argument's sake if you could earn 6% a year in a tax free fixed deposit account, your $100 today would be worth $106 in one year. This dramatically illustrates the maxim that 'time is money'. Another way of looking at it would be to factor in the effects of inflation and realise that because of the erosion of purchasing power caused by that major economic blight, once again $100 today buys more than $100 tomorrow. If inflation runs at 4%, the same basket of goods you can buy for $100 in the market today, will cost you $104 in 365 days. This change over time means that time itself has some monetary worth if you start with any sum of cash. (See also **DCF**.)

time to maturity
The remaining lifespan of a **bond**.

tip
A speculator is constantly looking for a hot tip or story to allow for a quick dollar to be made. These are generally passed along verbally and are usually not worth the paper they are written on!

tipster
One who passes on a **tip**.

TOPIX Index
The primary index of the Tokyo Stock Exchange usually disregarded by the global investment community in favour of the **Nikkei-225**.

total return
The full gain made on an **investment** in a set period. For instance if a **stock** has been held for one year and if it has appreciated 20%, while yielding a 5% after tax **dividend**, the total return on that investment has been 25%.

trading range
The price band a **stock** moves within. For instance, if Volatile Inc. starts the week at $40 a share and fluctuates 10% in the days following, its trading range for that period would be $36 to $44 a share.

trading volume
The **volume** of a stock in a set period, usually a day or week.

tranche
If a new issue of **stock**s or **bond**s are staggered in several instalments, each one of these would be a tranche.

transaction
A deal involving the sale of an **investment** and the corresponding purchase.

transaction cost
How much it costs to do the deal. In countries with graduated commission scales, the per unit transaction cost for a large **block** of shares would be lower than for a transaction of just one **board lot**, for instance.

Transferable Subscription Right
TSR. (See **warrant**.)

Treasury bill
A short-term government security sold at a **discount** to its face value in competitive bidding. The quantum of the discount when considered with the tenure of the **T-bill** carry with them an implicit interest rate. The usual tenures are three to six months. In the US, these are auctioned every Monday. In the US, these are routinely referred to as US T-bills, standing obviously for **US Treasury bills**.

Treasury bond
A long-term government issued **bond** to finance government expenditure, usually with a tenure exceeding five years. In the US, **US Treasury bonds** are also used to help pay down the national debt but because the **bond**s themselves are debt instruments, the net effect of incurring long-term debt to pay off more current debt would appear to merely put off the final day of reckoning.

Treasury note
A mid-term government debt security to finance government expenditure. The usual tenure, particularly of **US Treasury notes** is one to five years.

Triffin dilemma
An economic problem foreseen in the late 1950s by Robert Triffin. He realised that the US was heading for trouble if it needed to act as the supplier of the de facto global currency, the US$, while also ensuring sufficient gold reserves to back all this **money** floating around. These twin responsibilities were foisted onto the US by the now defunct **Bretton Woods System**, and failed because the only way the US could provide global liquidity was to incur foreign liabilities.

TSE
Taiwan Stock Exchange.

TSE Weighted Price Index
The **benchmark index** of the **Taiwan Stock Exchange**.

TSR
Transferable Subscription Right. This is a tradable derivative instrument which allows an investor the right to buy a **stock** at a prescribed price within a stipulated time frame. (See **warrant**.)

TTF
Thai Fund.

turnaround
A company that begins to show new vigour after a protracted period of losses and drop in market share. This is a relatively rare phenomenon and when it does happen suggests a more able **board** steering the company aright, combined with improved economics.

turnover
Total sales for a **company**. Also, the appropriate **currency** value of the underlying securities making up **volume**.

TWN
Taiwan Fund.

U

U
The single letter code for US Air, a company listed on the **NYSE**. (See **stock symbol**.)

unappropriated profit
retained earnings.

uncovered option
naked option.

underlying investment
Basic foundation of any type of **option**. It can be a **stock** (see **underlying stock**), an **index**, a **bond**, any type of **currency** or even a **futures contract**.

underlying stock
Basic foundation of an equity **option**. It is the actual stock that will be bought or sold when an **option** is exercised. (See **underlying investment**.)

undermargined account
A **margin account** that no longer has sufficient **margin** within it to meet a broker's requirements.

Understanding KLCI Stock Index Futures

The definitive book by Fred KH Tam (Times Editions, 1996) on trading the Kuala Lumpur Options and Financial Futures Exchange's KLCI Stock Index Futures contract. Within it Tam elucidates 10 succinct rules on successful futures trading. (See **Tam, Fred KH** and **KLOFFE**.)

undervalued stock

Any stock trading below the break-up value of its constituent assets or its fair market value, as ascertained by **financial analysts.** This second, less quantifiable criterion, of an undervalued stock is extremely open to subjective calls of **investment** judgment.

underwriter

Unlike an undertaker whose role is played at the end of his customer's life, an underwriter plays his role at the beginning of a **stock** or **bond** issue's life. The **underwriting body** guarantees a minimum level of subscription to the new issue and literally undertakes (hence the term) to cover any shortfall arising from insufficient investor interest.

underwriting body

A merchant bank or stock brokerage that provides underwriting services. (See **underwriter**.)

unit trust

Although the term is often used interchangeably with a **mutual fund**, a unit trust is similar only to an open-end mutual fund and not a **closed-end fund**. As such, its price moves strictly in line with the **NAV** of its **portfolio** and not directly because of **demand and supply** conditions brought about by its unit holders buying or selling the unit trust. (See **open-end fund**.)

uptick
When the last price done on a stock is above the one before.

uptrend
A situation of rising prices.

US GAAP
Also merely called **GAAP**.

US Treasury bills
See **Treasury bill**.

US Treasury bonds
See **Treasury bond**.

US Treasury notes
See **Treasury note**.

usury
Prohibitively high, and therefore morally unjustifiable, rate of **interest**. Consider the 10% *per month* interest often charged by illegal loan sharks in every country in Asia. On a compounded basis, that works out to an **APR** of 214%, clearly a usurious rate of interest.

utility
Any company involved in supplying basic infrastructure requirements like electricity, gas, water, telecommunication facilities and postal services.

In economics it is also a general term for the usefulness derived from owning an **asset**.

utilities
General term for **utility** companies.

V

The single letter code for Vivra, a company listed on the **NYSE**. (See **stock symbol**.)

variance

A statistical measure of risk that examines the extent of spreading around a mean. The higher the variance, the greater the **volatility** of the security, a **stock**, for example, being examined.

vendors' shares

Shares owned by current major shareholders of a **company**, usually about to list, that are offered to the public as part of the **IPO** exercise. The vendors' shares and the new shares issued for the public offer together make up the pool of **stock** made available to the general investment community.

volatility

In general terms, merely the price fluctuation of an **investment** over time. However for those who prefer to pin down their definitions, the realm of statistics defines volatility as the **standard deviation** of the return or price of a security.

volume

The total number of shares or **bond**s traded in a period, usually a day. This is linked to **turnover** by the simple relationship:

$$\text{volume} = \frac{\text{turnover}}{\text{weighted average price of the security for the period}}$$

W

W
The single letter code for Westvaco, a company listed on the **NYSE**. (See **stock symbol**.)

W3
WWW.

wadiah
In countries that practice Islamic banking, this term refers to the depositing of an **asset** with a bona fide party that nonetheless is not the owner of the asset.

Wall Street
Specifically the name of a street in New York City that dates back to a time when a wall had to be constructed to protect the white settlers from Amerindian attacks. Now it denotes the general Manhattan area housing the **NYSE** that is the financial hub of the US and by extension, of the whole world. (For the NYSE address see anecdote within the **Efficient Market Theory** entry.)

warrant
A piece of paper issued by a **company** that gives its owner the right to apply for new **common shares** in that company at a set price within a stipulated period, usually within five years of the warrant issue. If a warrant comes with loan stock but is itself detachable it is also called a **transferable subscription right** (**TSR**).

wasting asset
Unlike an appreciating one, a wasting asset drops in value with time. For a prime example, see **option**.

Weak Form Efficiency
The type of price efficiency inherent in an arena exhibiting the **Weak Form of the Efficient Market Theory**.

Weak Form of the Efficient Market Theory
States that prices of a **common stock** are independent of each other, which implies that past prices have no predictive power over future prices. This concurs with the **Random Walk Theory**. The investment world is clearly split down the middle (between fundamental and technical-based analysts) as to the applicability of the Weak Form. (See **Efficient Market Theory** and **Weak Form Efficiency**.)

weak market
A sustained declining market where sellers are more aggressive in offloading than buyers are in biting. (See **bear market**.)

wedge
When a stock's price begins to oscillate in an ever tighter band, and the price chart of its travels between successive highs and lows begins to resemble a tapering slice of cake.

weighted average number of common shares
The number of shares of any listed company is not a static figure. Companies can issue shares in the course of a year for many reasons,

such as a **rights issue** to shareholders or in consideration of an acquisition. In the US buy-backs are also possible where a company repurchases some of its shares from the market, thus *reducing* the number available. So to ensure a fair comparison between apples and apples (and not some sneaky members of the citrus clan) commonly used yardsticks like **EPS** and **DPS** must be divided by the average number of shares for the year in question.

This widely used denominator is 'weighted' by time. For instance, if company Obese Ltd has a financial year that corresponds to the calendar year, let's track its expansion of its **equity base**.

Jan 1
Obese starts the year with 100m shares.

April 1
It then issues 10m new shares for the acquisition of a start-up health company, Anorexic Ltd.

July 1
Obese completes a 1-for-2 rights issue, with all 55m new issues issued on this date.

> This is how the weighted average number of common shares for the entire year is worked out.
> For 3 months Obese had 100m shares.
> For another 3 months, 110m.
> For the last 6 months of the year, 165m shares.

The weighted average number of common shares =
$$\{(3 \times 100) + (3 \times 110) + (6 \times 165)\}/12 = 135m$$

This means that if in the course of the year, net earnings amounts to $67.5m, its **EPS** based on the weighted number of shares would be $0.50.

W-formation
The opposite of an **M-formation**. See **double bottom**.

'what's the news?'
Rumours, please!

White Knight
When an **asset stripper** or **greenmailer** shows up on the horizon, the **board** of the target company might seek out another company controlled by friendly parties to take a stake in the target company to foil the dastardly intentions of the predator. This rescuer is seen as a White Knight.

winding up
liquidation.

window dressing
Outright manipulation of a **company**'s **account**s to make them look better than they actually are, or merely over-emphasising positive points and downplaying negative numbers in the accounts toward the same purpose.

Although all listed companies are required by law to have external auditors vet their accounts to ensure a 'true and fair view' is reflected, since the auditors are appointed by the company's board and as the auditors' income is derived from retaining clients, there have been celebrated cases where true objectivity was sacrificed at the altar of year-end bonuses.

So a **savvy** investor learns to look beyond the window dressing at what is actually happening in the company through a thorough understanding of what the numbers truly signify.

The term 'window dressing' is also used to include the monkey business **fund manager**s have been known to get up to in the last few minutes of the last day of each reporting cycle when a few judicious low volume orders can push up the price of major holdings of their funds so as to artificially boost their performance numbers against their respective benchmark indices.

wire house
Any brokerage firm that is linked electronically to its branches, be they across a country or whole continents, for the rapid dissemination of information and orders.

wire transfer
An electronic transfer of funds from one bank to another.

Won
The name of the currencies of both North Korea and South Korea, though they are not equivalent with roughly 400 South Korean won being the equivalent of 1 North Korean won. (See **currencies**.)

working capital
Money used by a business to see it through normal expansion and regular business activities. It is specifically defined as:

working capital = current assets − current liabilities

World Bank
A sister multi-lateral organisation of the **IMF**, also based in Washington DC. Its official, though seldom used name, is The International Bank for Reconstruction and Development.

World Wide Web
Often erroneously used to mean the **Internet**. It is merely a (powerful) application on the Net to help navigate this globe-spanning resource that includes a vast store of **investment** information.

write down
An accounting exercise that puts through a perceived loss in value of an asset in a company's accounts. If carried to extremes, it may

result in a one-time **big bath** hit. After a write down, the **asset** is reflected in the **balance sheet** at its **written-down value**.

write off
An uncollectible **debt** that is given up as bad.

writer
The seller of a **put** or **call** option contract who helps make the options market by assuming the obligation to either sell the **underlying investment** of a call option or buy the underlying investment of a put option, at the relevant option's **exercise price**.

writer of a covered option
The person who already owns the **underlying investment**, and then sells **option**s on it. Since he already owns the underlying investment his potential loss in case the underlying hits the exercise price is either the cost of buying offsetting options or the opportunity cost (not actual out of pocket loss) of having to relinquish his **asset** at a price worse than that of the current market.

writer of a naked option
The person who does not own the **underlying investment** of his **option**. He may well be left with nothing on his back if his bet on the direction of the underlying investment is wrong, as he will need to go into the market and buy the underlying at the prevailing market price to cover the obligations assumed in writing his naked option. The cost could run into millions.

written-down value
The accounting value of an **asset** that has gone through a **write down**.

Wu Jiesi
Shenzen, China's Vice-Mayor with a progressive track record. His efforts are deemed instrumental in the remarkable growth seen on

the **Shenzen Securities Exchange**. To quote the **Far Eastern Economic Review** of September 5, 1996:

> (His) efforts are earning him a heroic reputation in Chinese financial circles. "He's young, capable, enjoys good relationships with the government bureaus in Beijing, and is very familiar with market economies," marvels (a) senior securities-firm official. "He was working so hard he spit up blood during a meeting in Hong Kong." (p. 62, 'The Battle of the Bourses'.)

WWW
World Wide Web.

X

x
ex.

x
The single letter code for USX, a company listed on the **NYSE**. (See **stock symbol**.)

xa
ex-all.

xb
ex-bonus or ex-capitalisation.

xc
ex-capitalisation or ex-bonus.

xd
ex-dividend.

xr
ex-rights.

xw
ex-warrants.

Y

Y
The single letter code for Alleghany, a company listed on the **NYSE**. (See **stock symbol**.)

Yangtze Region Development Fund
See **YRDF**.

yankee bond
A **bond** issued by non-US entities denominated in US dollars for the ease of US investors. (See **samurai bond**.)

Year-on-Year
A comparison of economic or financial data that looks at the percentage change over the preceding 12-month period. For instance, **Y-o-Y** increase in car sales of 10% in May, 1997, means that one-tenth more cars were sold in May, 1997, than were sold in May, 1996. (See **Month-on-Month**.)

Year to date
Same as **Year-on-Year**. (See **Month to date**.)

Yen
The Japanese currency. (See **currencies**.)

yield
Generally, the percentage return on an **investment**.

For **bond**s, this shows the actual rate of earnings from this debt instrument. It is easily calculated by taking the **coupon rate** of the bond and dividing it by its current price, and is denoted in percentage terms.

For **common stock**, as there is no comparable maturity period, the yield is simply its current annual **dividend** divided by its price.

yield curve
A graph plotting the relationship between the **yield to maturity** and various maturities (ranging from short-term to long-term) of **bond**s that are identical in every other respect. Same as **term structure of interest rates**.

yield to call
For some bonds that can be bought back by the issuer at staggered call dates, the yield to call refers to the **IRR** of a **bond** if it is only held from the present to the next call date.

yield to maturity
The **IRR** of a **bond** if held from the present to its **maturity date** which gives a measure of the bond's value at any point in time. At the time of its issue, working out the yield to maturity involves compounding the rate of return on the initial purchase price of a bond over its entire life.

Y-o-Y
Year-on-Year. (See **M-o-M**.)

YRDF
Yangtze Region Development Fund. This **SITIC**-run fund is primarily involved in direct infrastructure investment, though it will invest part of its **capital** in **Class A equities**.

Yuan
The Chinese domestic currency equivalent to the **Renminbi**. (See **currencies**.)

Z

Z
The single letter code for Woolworth, a company listed on the **NYSE**. (See **stock symbol**.)

zero coupon bond
Bonds sold at a steep discount to their **nominal value** but with no **coupon rate** attached. (See **pure discount bond**.)

zero-plus tick
This describes a situation when the last price done on a **stock** is the same as the previous trading price, which in turn had been an increase. For instance if ABC Ltd's last four stock trades were at $3.10, $3.20, $3.20 and $3.00, the second $3.20 could be described as a zero-plus tick. (See **uptick**.)

zero sum game
An attempt to beat the averages in a **zero sum market**.

zero sum market
A market like financial futures and options where, *at any one point in time*, any loss made by a **market player** is offset by a corresponding, equal, gain by another.

ABOUT THE AUTHOR

Rajen Devadason is a card-carrying member of Mensa UK who has been a Malaysia-based financial journalist since 1990. He graduated in 1988 with a BSc (Honours) in Physics and Computing from King's College, University of London. He has worked as a TV English language newscaster for Malaysia's TV3; a trainee chartered accountant with KPMG Peat Marwick in the UK; an investment analyst with (the then) Standard Chartered Securities in KL; as the primary Malaysian stringer for *Time* magazine; and a business puzzle columnist for *The Sun* in Malaysia.

As a staff writer for *Malaysian Business* magazine, he won the 1993 Malaysian Press Institute's award for best economic journalism. He was also named the 1993 Malaysian winner of the Citibank Pan-Asia business journalism award and in 1994 was the country's sole representative in a related seminar at New York's Columbia University, which included visits to the White House, the New York Fed and the World Bank.

He lives in Seremban, 40 miles south of KL, where he now runs his own writing business under the tag RD Book Projects. He is also contributing editor to *Smart Investor*, contributing reporter to *Asiaweek*, and a columnist for *Malaysian Business* magazine. *Your A–Z Guide to the Stock Market* is his first book. He is currently working on his next one, on life and financial planning.